Grades K–6

Everyday Mathematics®

Home Connection Handbook

A Guide for Administrators and Teachers

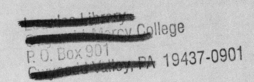

McGraw Hill **Wright Group**

The McGraw·Hill Companies

Contributors
Regina Anderson, Ellen Dairyko, Pamela Dayhoff, Mary Jo Hustoles,
Dr. Marci Larsen, Dr. Shahrzad Mahootian, Sheryl O'Connor,
Peg Rangel, Kim Sitzberger, Barbara Smart

Wright Group

Printed in the United States of America.

Send all inquiries to:
Wright Group/McGraw-Hill
P.O. Box 812960
Chicago, IL 60681

ISBN 0-07-600074-5

8 9 10 11 POH 09 08 07 06 05

The **McGraw·Hill** Companies

Contents

Introduction to the Home Connection Handbook

Throughout the *Home Connection Handbook,* you will read how important it is to build communication lines between home and school. Without family support, understanding, and encouragement, your job as teacher will be more difficult. This handbook has been prepared as a tool for teachers to use as they communicate with parents. It contains ideas and strategies for communicating that first year of implementation, as well as ideas for continuing communication growth after the initial year. If the communication habit is established early and often, parents will learn about the philosophy of the program, they will see how it works on a regular basis, and they will see that their children are successful. And that's the bottom line for us all, whether we are parent or teacher (and sometimes both!)—mathematical success for our children and our students.

The Essay portion of the *Handbook* is specifically addressed to you, the teacher. Each essay looks at a different situation—new teachers, new parents, experienced parents and teachers, and so on. The remainder of the *Handbook* provides resources to share with parents that will make it easier for you to explain some of the key features of the program. Always remember that your goal is to include parents as part of the teaching team.

*E*ssays for Teachers of Everyday Mathematics

Each of the articles in this section is authored by one of your *Everyday Mathematics* colleagues. Each article contains suggestions for building communication between school and home. You'll find consensus in many areas. For example, all authors stress that the rewards of reaching out to parents far outweigh the time needed to establish those relationships. Several authors discuss Math Night activities and the overwhelmingly positive responses from parents when they do the activities themselves. And all authors discuss how enthusiasm and interest in school flow from teachers to parents and children and then back to teachers again.

As you read, keep in mind that you have just as many great ideas; one of the richest resources within your reach is your colleagues. Most teachers are eager to share their ideas and methods.

Kindergarten Everyday Mathematics: *First-Year Teachers and First-Year Parents*

Communicating with parents is one of the key ingredients to the successful implementation of the *Everyday Mathematics* (EM) program in your classroom. As a kindergarten teacher, you have a very important and sometimes challenging task. Open the lines of communication by focusing on the one thing all parents have in common: *They want their children to receive the* **BEST** *education possible.* Let parents know that you consider them an integral part of their child's educational team.

How do you tell parents about a program that is new to you as well? It isn't as difficult as you might expect. Parents need to know the history and philosophy behind the EM program in order to understand and support it. You may do that in a number of ways.

Fall Open House Math Night

- Make a list of the points that impressed you as you were learning about the program.
- Make a transparency, poster, or handout containing the kindergarten EM viewpoint found on page viii of the Kindergarten *Program Guide and Masters* book.
- Play a math game with your parents, or let the parents rotate at math centers that have different games and math manipulatives. This will give parents a hands-on idea of *what* is being taught, *how* it is being taught, and *why* it is being taught this way. **Keep it simple and fun!** Your parents will leave with a more open and positive attitude toward the program. Choose activities, games, and explorations that have already been introduced and played at the time of your open house. For example, try Partner Match, page 12; Coins in the Classroom, page 15; Pattern Blocks, page 16; Listen and Count, page 21; and Eating to Zero, page 22.

Pam Dayhoff

Pam has been in primary education for the past 15 years. She is currently the Primary Math Specialist for the Temple Independent School District in Temple, Texas.

How do you tell parents about a program that is new to you as well? It isn't as difficult as you might expect.

Most parents appreciate regular communication between the classroom and the home because their children may not be very forthcoming when asked, "What did you learn in school today?"

Letters

- Our principal added a letter in our *Parent-Student Handbook* that explained the reasons behind the decision to adopt the EM program.
- Make an EM family packet that includes letters from the district or principal as well as the articles and hand-outs included in this *Home Connection Handbook*.
- There is an excellent example of an initial letter in the *Program Guide and Masters Book*. Read and adapt the letter to meet your needs.

Product Communication

product (pro'dekt) *n*. 1. Anything produced by labor.

Kindergarten EM is an activity-based program where the children create many products—patterns, graphs, measurement, sorting, and so on. Parents should know that a product is *anything* made by the child. For example,

- Symmetry with paints, page 61
- Fold-and-cut projects, page 65
- Order-of-Daily Events, page 160
- Macaroni Necklaces, page 165
- Bead String Name Collections, page 231
- Making a pattern using buttons, shoes, and so on
- Playing a math game
- Counting shapes in the house
- Sorting and graphing a bag of colored candies

Suggestion: Our school now has a digital camera. We take pictures of the children with their finished products and include these pictures in our weekly/monthly newsletters. What a great motivator—parents can't wait to read the newsletters, and children love to see themselves in the newsletters!

Ongoing Communication

Most parents appreciate regular communication between the classroom and the home because their children may not be very forthcoming when asked, "What did you learn in school today?"

- *Weekly or monthly newsletters*
Keep your parents informed about what is going on in class and ways they can help their children at home. You can review what has been taught and give parents a "heads up" on present and future projects and games and any upcoming events (such as Math Game Night, 100th Day Celebration, and so on).

- *Mathtime Helpers*
Invite parents to your classroom. Make it fun for them, and they'll come back! Some parents may prefer just observing. As helpers or observers, parents will leave with a higher appreciation and respect for the program, the teacher, and their children's ability.

Communicating with parents is an important step in our main objective—teaching our children math. We all want our children to be competent and confident in their ability to do and understand mathematics. Parents need to know that math is everywhere—everyday— and that it is challenging, stimulating, and fun.

Kindergarten: Parent Communication After Your First Year

Congratulations! You've completed at least one year teaching kindergarten *Everyday Mathematics* (EM). Although you have a year behind you, every year is the first year of EM for your kindergarten parents; therefore, home communication is essential. The ultimate goal of home communication is to help parents consciously integrate "math talk" and math activities into their child's daily life. Plan for a variety of methods. Try to remember some of the questions you had when you were new to EM. Your kindergarten parents will have many of those same questions too.

Parent Nights

Schedule a meeting early in the school year to discuss grade-level curriculum and student learning expectations. The math portion of the meeting should provide background information and a brief discussion on kindergarten EM's design, content strands, daily routines, and goals. Follow this up by having parents participate in a few activities, such as these.

• Warm up by asking Minute Math question #7, "What numbers have you seen?" Then ask, "How have you used numbers today?" Chart or graph parent responses, and share the chart or graph with your students the following day.
• Prepare a short presentation, including overheads, of children doing math activities to illustrate major points.

Open House—Parents and Students

An open house is usually informal and allows for only the briefest curriculum discussion. Here are a few ideas for showing EM at work.

• Display pictures, with captions, of children involved in math activities.
• Set out a few math activities, labeled with directions, and have children teach their parents.
• Display the kindergarten EM Content-by-Strand poster. The back of the poster details the learning goals for the entire school year.

Barbara Smart

Barbara is a kindergarten teacher in Portage Public Schools, Portage, Michigan. She has been a K–5 classroom teacher and reading specialist for 30 years. Barbara has served in both reading and mathematics curriculum leadership positions.

The ultimate goal of home communication is to help parents consciously integrate "math talk" and math activities into their child's daily life.

Product and Ongoing Communication

Many teachers, including myself, feel that ongoing parent communication is just as important—perhaps more important—than a one-time night meeting.

• *Newsletters*
Provide parents with information, and then give them ideas on how they can work with their children at home. For example, "During the past week, we have been working with coin recognition and value with pennies, nickels, and dimes. In order to reinforce these concepts at home, empty your pockets, and have your child identify the coins. Talk about each coin's value, and make trades (such as five pennies for one nickel). You may also wish to count by ones, fives, and tens using the coins available."

• *Home Links Booklets*
Home Links booklets are a great communication tool. Distribute them to parents early in the year or at fall or spring conferences.

• *Bulletin Board Displays*
Display student math work, class charts, and graphs. Try using products created from the following activities from the kindergarten *Teacher's Guide to Activities:* page 61, Symmetry with Paints; page 73, Shape Designs; and page 105, Paper-Folding Geometry.

• *Parent Teacher Conferences*
Put a few games, student-created products such as math books, and classmade charts and graphs next to a math bulletin board. Add photos of students engaged in math activities, and your parents will see kindergarten EM in action.

Share checklists, products saved from math activities, anecdotal records, and any specific skills testing as part of your conference. The combination of sources will help provide a broad picture of a child's progress.

Grades One–Three: Your First Year

So … you are implementing *Everyday Mathematics* this year! Teachers working with a new curriculum are excited, yet often feel overwhelmed about the prospect of familiarizing themselves with new content, terminology, preparation, and, perhaps, teaching styles, along with everything else that accompanies the beginning of a new school year. A wonderful, yet often underused, asset to many teachers is the parent community. Most parents wish to be involved in their child's learning, and this parental support can assist in creating an environment where exploring, learning, and using math is engaging and meaningful to children. The key to getting and keeping parents involved in a collaborative manner is communication.

Getting Off to a Good Start

At the beginning of the implementation process, send home the Family Letter found at the beginning of the Home Links section in the grade level *Math Masters* book. It is called "Introduction to First Grade (or Second Grade or Third Grade) *Everyday Mathematics*." This letter includes the various content strands, some of the terminology used, and the components of the program.

Set a date for your school's Back-to-School/Curriculum Overview Night. I recommend this evening take place within the first three weeks of school. At this time, you may give a more in-depth presentation of *Everyday Mathematics*. If your school does not hold such an event or if there is not much time to cover the new math curriculum, you might think about holding a Math Night. You can distribute a letter like the sample on page 8 prior to the first day or within the first few days of school.

Ellen Dairyko

Ellen has taught in the Chicago Public Schools for 26 years and has been using Everyday Mathematics *in her first-grade classroom for 12 years. She worked closely with the program authors at the beginning stages of the project and helped write the first editions of* Everyday Mathematics *for first, second, and third grades.*

Remember, you are new to the curriculum! You may not know all the answers! Assure your audience you will research the answer and get back to them as soon as you can.

FROM THE CLASSROOM OF:
Mrs. Dairyko

Dear Parents,

Welcome to _____ grade! I am excited about meeting you and your child on Tuesday, August 22! I am also delighted to inform you that we will be working with a new math program called *Everyday Mathematics*.

Everyday Mathematics is a comprehensive curriculum that follows the National Council of Teachers of Mathematics (NCTM) standards. See the attached Introduction to *Everyday Mathematics* Family Letter for additional details of the program.

Our Back-to-School Night is scheduled for _____. At that time, I will present a more in-depth picture of *Everyday Mathematics*. I hope to see all of you there!

Sincerely,
Mrs. Dairyko

Sample Cover Letter

Most parents wish to be involved in their child's learning, and this parental support can assist in creating an environment where exploring, learning, and using math is engaging and meaningful to children.

Back-to-School Math Night

Remember, you are new to the curriculum! You may not know all the answers! Assure your audience you will research the answer and get back to them as soon as you can. I highly recommend that prior to your parent meeting, you utilize the resources found in the *Teacher's Lesson Guide* and the *Teacher's Reference Manual* for clarification of concepts introduced and reviewed throughout *Everyday Mathematics*. Much of the material will be helpful in answering your questions and those of your parents.

Sample Activities for a Back-to-School Math Night

- Begin your evening with an estimation activity. (How many pennies or jellybeans, buttons, noodles are in this jar?) After parents jot down estimates, save them until the end of your presentation.
- Give a brief overview—no more than five minutes—of the philosophy of *Everyday Mathematics*.
- Describe how children are encouraged not only to solve problems but to share the thought process that leads to the solutions.
- Point out that throughout the primary grades, understanding the concepts behind basic facts and procedures is equally as important as mastering the basic facts.
- Explain that concepts are revisited frequently during the year and throughout the K–6 cycle— and not to expect children to master money, time, basic facts, and so on, the first time around.
- Post the *Everyday Mathematics* Content by Strand chart, and invite parents to examine it at their leisure. The chart presents on one page the math concepts covered throughout the year.
- Describe the components and how they are used throughout the day. Have samples available for parents to examine.
- Explain that the journals are records of the children's math studies throughout the year and that journals will not be sent home until they are finished. Invite parents to come into the classroom to look through their children's math journals.

- Demonstrate a few beginning games. For example, for first grade, Number Line Squeeze, Top-It, or Penny/Dice Game; for second grade, Addition Top-It, Money Exchange Game, or Broken Calculator; for third grade, Beat the Calculator or Name That Number.
- Elicit support from parents to replay these and other games that are sent home throughout the year. Encourage volunteers to assist with activities in the classroom.
- Explain that you will be sending home a regular letter that will present a "big-picture" overview of the units and lessons.
- Wrap up the evening by completing the estimation activity. Ask a few volunteers to share their estimates and how they arrived at them. Ask if anyone used a different strategy. Point out that the children in your class are being challenged to share their thinking in much the same way.

Ongoing Communication

- Use letters to remind parents not to overdo practice activities at home. Parents and children work best together when activities are enjoyable rather than tedious.
- Keep your letters informative, yet short—no more than one page. This will increase the chances that your parents will take the time to read them! A letter that summarizes a week's worth of math activities can be short (as shown above), or it can be longer (as shown on page 10).

Remember, it doesn't hurt to repeat yourself now and then in your communications with parents. They may need to hear your ideas and suggestions several times before they act upon them!

FROM THE CLASSROOM OF: Mrs. Dairyko

Dear Parents,

Hope you've had a great week. Here's our weekly "Short Report" to let you know what your children have been doing in *Everyday Mathematics* this week.

We continued working with patterns in numbers. We found the distances between numbers on the number grid. We also counted by 2s, 5s, and 10s on the number grid.

Sincerely,
Mrs. Dairyko

Brief summary of math for the week

Product Communication

There are a number of products, or items, produced by the children as they work with *Everyday Mathematics*. Math Boxes and Home Links are fairly easy to check, comment on, and send home on a regular basis for parents to review with their children. Often products from Projects and Explorations are visible artifacts of math activities from the classroom. I make displays of these products and, as an added activity, have the children write about how they made them. After a short time, I send them home with the accompanying explanations.

When children write number stories, I often post them on the bulletin boards so the school community can enjoy them. I do not require the children to edit them (unless that is our writing goal), so the pages may have spelling and grammatical errors in them. It's also fun and fairly easy to assemble the number story pages into class booklets for home circulation. I have found that assembling

FROM THE CLASSROOM OF:
Mrs. Dairyko

Dear Parents,

Hope you've had a great week. We were **very** busy this week, and I want to let you know what we've been doing in math.

We made an hour-hand-only clock and practiced telling time to the hour. We also spent time examining pennies, nickels, and dimes. Every child should have 5 nickels and 6 dimes from home to use during math. This money is stored in your child's toolkit money holder and will be used throughout the year.

Next week I will send a Home Link home with students, asking for 2 quarters. Counting money is a skill that develops with practice. A game that will help your child is called "Penny, Nickel Exchange Game." Players make a "bank" of 40 pennies and 10 nickels. Players take turns rolling a die and collecting that number of pennies from the bank. As players acquire 5 or more pennies, they say "exchange" and turn in 5 pennies for a nickel. The game ends when the bank is empty. Players count the amount of money they have and play again if they wish.

The children played the above game this week. Next week they will add dimes and play the "Penny, Nickel, Dime Exchange Game."

Sincerely,
Mrs. Dairyko

Longer summary of math
for the week

booklets such as these throughout the year results in a wonderful running record of the children's grasp of mathematical concepts, as well as the development of their writing skills. The children are very proud to share their work, and parents get a glimpse of the number story process. This idea can be extended to algorithms that children have invented, Math Boxes, Frames and Arrows, Name-Collection Boxes, What's My Rule?, and other routines. If you have children write about their math thinking, compile the writings into booklets to share with parents.

As a first-year *Everyday Mathematics* teacher, you have a busy year ahead of you. The support, understanding, and collaboration of your parents will go a long way toward ensuring that your first year (and successive years) will be exciting and fulfilling mathematical journeys with your students!

Grades One–Three: After Your First Year

The anticipation of a new school year is always exciting, and the need to keep parents informed of their child's curriculum is an important task in the fall. This is easily accomplished through a parent letter. The letter could list a brief summary of the mathematical strands that were previously introduced to students, along with the repeated exposures to these strands students will encounter in the current school year. An example might include the following: "In second grade, your child read and wrote numbers through 10,000. In third grade, this will be extended to reading, writing, and ordering numbers to 1,000,000."

An open house is another opportunity to display projects such as the Sunrise/Sunset Chart in the third-grade program or Boxes, Boxes, Delightful Boxes in first- and second-grade classrooms. Displaying photographs of Exploration Centers, which students from the year before worked on, demonstrates the open-ended learning opportunities students will experience in the upcoming school year. If there are any parents in your room new to *Everyday*

Mathematics, you could provide information from previous years to introduce them to the program.

Keeping parents informed about their own child's performance is supported in several ways using Journal Pages, Math Boxes, and Home Links, as well as the end-of-unit assessments. Individual journal pages can be copied and sent home, accompanied by a note of celebration or concern. A journal page can even enhance some of the Home Links sent home to provide parents with additional information regarding a new routine, such as Frames and Arrows. When making journal page selections, be sure to clarify content to parents in order to communicate information about their child's progress.

Decisions on how best to use Math Boxes vary from grade level to grade level; however, the blank cells in a Math Box can be used to review concepts students need or to encourage students to record concepts they know. For example, if students list the math facts they know in an empty cell of a Math Box, parents and teachers could assess that child's self-confidence in the area of operations. Blank

Mary Jo Hustoles

Mary Jo has been a teacher for 25 years in primary, secondary, and special education—although her first love is first grade! She has been a frequent consultant for Everyday Mathematics *since 1986. Mary Jo holds her Ed.S. from Minnesota State University, Mankato, where she also has been an adjunct professor.*

Displaying photographs of Exploration Centers, which students from the year before worked on, demonstrates the open-ended learning opportunities students will experience in the upcoming school year.

Math Box templates can be found in the *Math Masters* books. Look on the following pages:
- Grade One—pages 141-142
- Grade Two—pages 217-219
- Grade Three—page 199

Home Links can be adjusted to meet the communication needs your particular school may already have established with your parent population. For example, if your school sends home a folder every Tuesday, adjust your Home Links to accommodate that schedule. Consider sending home a packet of all the Home Links for that week's lessons or a selection of Home Links from previous lessons. The goal of Home Links has always been to make parents an equal partner and an ally in the math learning process.

Unit assessments may not stand alone as a clear message to parents of student progress. The Individual Profiles of Progress from the *Assessment Handbook* can assist you in your communication about specifics. Select from your unit assessment a concept or skill that is aligned with a unit goal. Use the language on the Individual Profiles of Progress to provide parents with a goal statement about their child's progress. A first-grade example may say "Mary is *secure* in making tally marks for the numbers 9 and 16; however, she is *developing* in her ability to fill in missing numbers in a sequence of 1–20."

Use $1\frac{1}{2}$- by 2-inch sticky notes to control your anecdotal recording about students. Choose a singular area of behavior, such as "cooperative group behavior," and watch each child during the math learning games the program supports. Use the Beginning, Developing, and Secure Rubric to assess each child's status. Record the date, and trans-

fer the sticky note to a numbered page for each child. Put your students in alphabetical order, and assign a personal number for each child. A finished note might look like the one on the far left.

The interpretation quickly shows the date, the student's number, the behavior being observed (cooperative group behavior, or CGB) and a brief note (S: Takes turns). This recording provides the teacher with data for each student within a class period. Several observations of "cooperative group behavior" will help both parents and teachers see a pattern of behavior of students within a group setting.

Student self-assessments can provide compelling depth about a student's knowledge of a topic. A "question of the day," such as a Math Message, can yield great insight.

The key to success with parents is to simply follow your ABCs:

Accommodate your parent's schedule.

Build a relationship of trust.

Communicate, communicate, communicate!

10/21/99

#4

CGB

S: Takes turns

The key to success with parents is to simply follow your ABCs:

Accommodate your parent's schedule.

Build a relationship of trust.

Communicate, communicate, communicate!

Grades Four–Six: The First Year

"Students, do the uneven problems on page 101 and have your parents help you on the harder word problems at the bottom of the page. Remember, Friday is the big test."

After 25 years of making such assignments, I changed from traditional texts to the *Everyday Mathematics* program. The district concluded that this program would better meet the needs of this student population. I, as the teacher, was required to implement the change. A cornerstone of this program is excellent communication between teacher, student, and parent—for the benefit of the student!

Role of Teacher—Raise your Comfort Level

1. Get Trained! The New User's Training is absolutely essential. It provides both the research behind and the philosophical basis of the program, as well as practical instruction using the program's components with teacher-trainers modeling successful techniques.

2. Study! Your *Teacher's Reference Manual* will provide you with the mathematical background for the lessons. The unit organizers and lesson plans in the *Teacher's Lesson Guides* will aid in the approach to teaching the program.

3. Collaborate! Find out what questions other teachers are hearing from parents. The more you know, the more confident you'll feel and, in turn, the more confident parents will feel. Good preparation will significantly lessen the intimidation factor resulting from a change in the method of instruction.

4. Teach! Use the *Everyday Mathematics* program as designed—without supplement—for at least one full school year. Pace your teaching to cover both journals within the school year, using the guidelines on the Content by Strand Chart.

5. Commit! Get behind the program 100 percent this year! If you give mixed messages now, you'll destroy this program with parents before you have the opportunity to demonstrate the program's tremendous benefits. Parent enthusiasm and participation are critical elements toward making the program work for you too.

Gina Anderson

Before relocating to Florida, Gina was a public school teacher in Missouri for 27 years. In 1998, she was chosen as one of six finalists for Missouri Teacher of the Year. She now teaches fifth grade at Saint Stephen's Episcopal School in Bradenton, Florida. She has been a consultant for Everyday Learning for four years.

Students will embrace the active learning involved in the discovery approach and will not miss the isolation and drill of the passive traditional math.

Everyday Mathematics changes the roles of teacher, student, and parent and with it, the teacher's professional responsibility to communicate to the family how this program works to benefit their child.

Role of Students— Good News!

Students will have little problem with this change to a new program. They will respond positively to a committed teacher and supportive parents. Students will embrace the active learning involved in the discovery approach and will not miss the isolation and drill of the passive traditional math.

Role of Parents—More Good News!

Parents will support a program they perceive as beneficial to their child even if they must adapt. They will support this change in organization and teaching not only because it better prepares their child for higher mathematics and makes him or her think, but because he or she is now learning before their eyes. This requires the teacher to communicate the essence of the program to parents. You must answer the parent's natural questions:

1. How does it work? Parents must understand what spiral learning is. The student no longer learns an isolated concept to mastery and then moves on with or without that skill. The scope and sequence of the program provides many opportunities for learning over a longer period of time.

2. How do you work this problem? Parents must understand the process of problem solving. A child's understanding is greatly improved when he or she discovers a solution to a problem rather than just applying a method provided by a textbook. The variety of algorithms will be a change, as will the lack of assignments from a textbook (such as "Do the odd numbered problems for homework.") and drill-and-practice worksheets.

3. Calculators? Yes, the use of calculators has been proven to increase, not decrease, understanding. The calculator is a useful tool in problem solving, but it does not replace the memorization of basic math facts.

4. Cooperative learning? Research shows cooperative learning will help children be better listeners and be better able to communicate their own ideas to others.

They will learn how to hear ideas that will help them build on their own ideas. Discussion groups are an important part of the learning process—and an important part of the workplace children will grow up to join.

5. When's the test? The concept of ongoing assessment versus the traditional test must be explained to parents. Although *Everyday Mathematics* does provide significant pen-and-paper assessment, it is the teacher's observation of the whole learning process that will give parents the true level of their child's performance.

Everyday Mathematics changes the roles of teacher, student, and parent and with it, the teacher's professional responsibility to communicate to the family how this program works to benefit their child. There are a number of methods and forums that can make communication more effective. These are shown on page 16.

Methods of Communication

Open House	Math Night	Parent Handbook
• Create a math display of the basic learning tools. • Have a group meeting, and enthusiastically introduce *Everyday Mathematics*. • Announce the date of Math Night, and advise parents to attend.	• Display samples of student work from previous years. • Involve parents in a participatory lesson and in a variety of games and activities. • Have parents use slates for mental math. • Explain the basic formats and terminology of *Everyday Mathematics*. • Emphasize ongoing home-school communication. • Invite parents to observe an actual lesson with the class. • Seek volunteers to help in the classroom. • Explain the benefits of ongoing assessment. • Distribute the *Parent Handbook*. (See next column.)	• Include the following from the *Home Connection Handbook:* a copy of the glossary, descriptions of algorithms, other information as needed. • Write a personal letter to parents that encourages them to communicate their concerns to you.
Communication through daily student routines	**Communication through students**	**Communication in writing**
• Use journals daily, and have parents sign them weekly. • Use Study Links, and be sure to send home other resources at appropriate times, such as Family Letters, the *Student Reference Book,* and so on. • Supply written instructions for all projects, and encourage parents to call with questions. • Respond immediately and positively to all parental notes on Journal or Study Link materials. • Encourage a dialogue with parents on the implementation of *Everyday Mathematics.*	• Send home an interesting algorithm from the daily lesson for students to explain to their parents, and have students write a paragraph describing their parents' response. • Send home game packs regularly for students to teach to and play with their parents and siblings. Have students complete a feedback sheet on the game pack.	• Use the Family Letters in the *Math Masters* for each unit. • Send home weekly newsletters that contain interesting activities done in math class. Praise students' efforts and achievements, and show examples of student's work.

Grades Four–Six: After Your First Year

Informed parents are extremely valuable partners in any student's education. Therefore, even after your first year of adopting *Everyday Mathematics,* it is as important as ever to continue communicating with your parents about math time in your classroom.

Program Communication

In fourth- through sixth-grade classrooms, some of the same questions may pop up repeatedly. Consider handing out "Frequently Asked Questions," found on pages 69 and 70 of this *Home Connection Handbook,* and the Family Letter "Introduction to XX Grade," found at the beginning of the Home Links section of the *Math Masters* book. In addition, you may want to have the *Content-by-Strand* and *Achievement Studies* booklets, as well as pictures of past student math projects, on display for parents to peruse.

One fear parents have is that they don't know enough about the math themselves to be able to help their child with math work. The intermediate-grade teachers at my school have offered parents the opportunity to purchase the *Student Reference Books* for their grade levels at Back-to-School Night so that parents can use this "math encyclopedia" at home when working with their children.

Product Communication

With a program such as *Everyday Mathematics,* where students are so directly involved in their own mathematical growth, there will be many products, or items, that each child creates as a result of their activities. Be sure to share these products with parents. For example, once students are secure in an algorithm, give them a problem, and have them explain in writing how they used their chosen algorithm to solve the problem. Most parents will be open to the various algorithms when they understand how they work and when they see their child using them successfully. Send home the algorithm section of this *Home Connection Handbook* (pages 49–58) to help parents get more clarification about algorithms.

Whenever a project is assigned, inform the parents ahead of time. Be clear in communicating what the students are expected to do in class and what they will be

Kim Sitzberger

Kim has taught fourth and fifth grades in CUSD 220 in Illinois for eight years. She has been an Everyday Mathematics *consultant for seven years.*

One fear parents have is that they don't know enough about the math themselves to be able to help their child with math work.

Remember, whenever possible, anticipate parent questions and be proactive. Parent-teacher communication is an ongoing investment in a child's journey to success. The support you receive from your educated parents will be well worth your efforts.

responsible for doing at home. Take pictures of the projects every year so that if students or parents have questions, you have real-life examples from previous years to show them.

Another way to showcase student products and learning is to leave Parent Math Night to the primary grades and replace the intermediate portion with the project tours. A Portfolio Day is also a great time for students to share their math progress with parents. Math portfolio items may include students' explanations of their chosen algorithms and a variety of reflection pages from the *Assessment Handbook*.

Ongoing Communication

Keep in touch with parents regularly. Parents will appreciate being informed about the daily math objectives. A great way to do this is to include in your classroom newsletter the Family Letters that are available at the beginning of every unit. If you send a regular newsletter, assign different students to write short articles about what they have learned in math since the last newsletter. Parents enjoy reading students' perspectives and will eagerly check to see if their child's article is in the newsletter.

Parents may express concern regarding the transition from *Everyday Mathematics* in fifth grade to the middle school math program if a different program is used at that level. Ease parents concerns by telling them you will send a letter about the different algorithms to the sixth-grade teachers so that students can continue using them in middle school. Hopefully, there will be strong communication about this issue in your district, and it will not be a serious issue after the first year. However, if this is not the case, send your math newsletters to the middle school teachers to keep them informed and to ensure a smooth transition for your students.

Remember, whenever possible, anticipate parent questions and be proactive. Parent-teacher communication is an ongoing investment in a child's journey to success. The support you receive from your educated parents will be well worth your efforts.

Everyday Mathematics:
What a Principal Has to Say

Congratulations! As the principal of a school implementing *Everyday Mathematics* (EM) you are in for an exciting year! If you have already implemented EM, you know what I am talking about. It is fascinating to watch teachers, students, and parents grow together in their mathematical know-how. However, none of that happens without someone making sure that each of the players has the right information, materials, and enthusiastic support. That someone is you—the elementary school principal!

When a school or district decides to make a change in curriculum, professional development usually focuses only on teachers. However, key to your long-term success will be to provide parents with "professional" development as well. So come along as I share my experiences in parent education and communication during a year in my life as an *Everyday Mathematics* principal!

May-June

While others' thoughts are filled with endings and plans for winding down, for a principal, this is just the beginning. Let parents know that a curriculum change has been or will be taking place. Using materials from the National Council of Teachers of Mathematics can give parents a background for changing how they think about mathematics.

This groundwork can also be laid by having teachers introduce EM games to students during May. This will establish the routine of games as an important part of mathematics. And by sending home some of the games for students to play over the summer, parents and students will begin thinking mathematically together.

July-August

Include information about *Everyday Mathematics* in a "welcome back" letter to parents. This gives them time to acclimate themselves to some of the upcoming changes as their children become proficient in thinking in the language of numbers. Teachers can incorporate information from the Family Letter provided by *Everyday Mathematics* for the beginning of each year. This letter is found in the *Math Masters* book. At our school, we have sent home directions to the game Top-It, with variations on how to play at all grade levels.

Sheryl O'Connor

Sheryl is the principal of a K–5 elementary school in Caledonia, Michigan, where she practices thinking mathematically with 330 of her favorite people. Mrs. O'Connor is married to a wonderful man, and they have two very spoiled dogs.

When a school or district decides to make a change in curriculum, professional development usually focuses only on teachers. However, key to your long-term success will be to provide parents with "professional" development as well.

Let parents know that the principal is a teacher too. Scheduling time to teach lessons at various grade levels, while scary, improves credibility for discussing implementation with both parents and staff.

Begin planning now for a Family Math Night. This provides an opportunity to distribute and discuss your customized *Parent Handbook*. The *Home Connection Handbook* contains many sections that can easily be copied and included in a parent handbook tailored specifically for your community. Including a letter of introduction from the superintendent or board members can underscore the district's commitment to increasing mathematical literacy through the use of *Everyday Mathematics*. Other suggestions are to include a glossary and examples and explanations of procedures and routines used in the *Everyday Mathematics* program that are new to parents.

September–October

Now that teachers have gotten their toes wet and students are beginning to experience math in a new light, it is time to branch out. All that planning for your Family Math Night will pay off.

- Invite parents to play games with their children. This will help parents understand the role of games in mastering fact power and developing the ability to communicate about strategies. "Name That Number" and "Getting to One" are excellent games for demonstrating the emphasis on mastery of number and operations sense.

- After playing the games, bring parents together to complete Number Stories About Egypt (from the fourth-grade *Math Masters* book, Study Link 3.5 on page 257) as examples of philosophy of rigorous content. It is eye-opening for parents to realize everyone doesn't have to

agree on how to get the answer in order to have in-depth math and skills practice. Once parents complete the measurements and discuss their own strategies, have them point out where they see rigorous content, learning conversations, and mathematical skills in the activity.

- Let parents know that the principal is a teacher too. Scheduling time to teach lessons at various grade levels, while scary, improves credibility for discussing implementation with both parents and staff. Not to mention the kids will love it!

November–December

Wow! The first semester is drawing to a close, and first-quarter report cards and parent teacher conferences are upon us. Consider how the changes in instruction will be reflected on report cards. Rather than changing report cards drastically, teachers could add an extra page. If report card changes have happened, consider having one person assigned to a help desk for parents during conferences. This person should be well versed in the changes and be able to explain the report card to parents.

January–February–March–April

Educators tend to get tunnel vision from winter to spring break. While everyone else is focused on the instruction of the moment, this is the principal's time to step back, refocus, and take a deep breath. It is time to make sure no information gaps exist.

- Make sure teachers are continuing to inform parents, especially when working on things like algorithms. Parents need to understand about the important move from repeating a defined algorithm to mastering number and operation sense.

- Recruit parents to help create games, make copies, play games with students who are struggling with fact power, and, most importantly, volunteer in classrooms. In first through third grades, parents helping with Explorations can make a huge difference to a teacher in the first year of implementation.

May-June

We're back to winding down—or in a principal's world, winding back up. Prepping for summer includes preparing for parents requesting summer work; game packets with a journal for recording strategies and results are one suggestion.

There you are! You have just completed your first year as an *Everyday Mathematics* principal. If the experience of others is any indication, you will be amazed at the growth of your students—even after only one year! Just as surprising will be the growth of mathematical literacy among the adults in your learning community. Teaching *Everyday Mathematics* is to model everyday learning. Enjoy!

Communicating from a Curriculum Coordinator's Perspective

Dr. Marci Larsen

Marci has worked in three school districts where Everyday Mathematics *has been implemented at the elementary level. She has been a principal, a curriculum director, and, most recently, an executive director for teaching and learning. Marci holds a doctorate in leadership and policy studies, a master's degree in school administration, and a bachelor's degree in special education.*

...if parents understand the Everyday Mathematics *program, they will not only want their children to participate in the program, they will insist upon it!*

I have worked in three school districts where *Everyday Mathematics* has been adopted and implemented—as a principal, then as curriculum director, and now as executive director for teaching and learning. In each of these positions, I have been involved in the beginning stages of implementation. What I have learned is what parents want for their children from our schools. They want their children to be safe, happy, and successful. Basically, they want what is best for their children. And if parents understand the *Everyday Mathematics* program, they will not only want their children to participate in the program, they will insist upon it!

As a principal, I had the delightful experience of having a parent of a former student return for a visit to discuss how to approach the junior high school staff about their math program. Her feeling was that after her son had participated in the *Everyday Mathematics* program at the elementary level, he was ready for more advanced work than was being offered at the junior high. An increase in student achievement at the elementary level provided the impetus necessary for changes to be made at the middle level!

To further understand how best to communicate with parents, remember that the only math most can relate to is the math they were taught; so their only hope of understanding this new program is through information from those who know and understand the program—the educators. When program materials are selected for use in a school district, teachers are typically highly involved over an extended period of time and learn about the underlying philosophy of the program. In addition, they learn about how the *Everyday Mathematics* program differs from more traditional programs. Parents haven't had these opportunities.

And it is amazing what students can do when given the EM opportunity. I vividly remember visiting a first-grade classroom where students were providing solutions for ways to get to a whole number and came up with negative numbers and fractions. They didn't call them negative numbers and fractions, but they obviously understood the concepts.

When thinking about communication, know that attitude makes a difference. If teachers and other staff are feeling positive about the program, that positive attitude is communicated to students and parents. If students are having a positive, successful experience with the program, they will communicate that success to their parents. It is our job to reinforce parental support!

For those teachers who feel unsure or have questions about any aspect of the program, they need to work through their issues and concerns with their colleagues. If this type of sharing happens with parents and students, be assured that those feelings of concern will be transferred to parents and students. For example, a common concern of teachers initially is the cyclical layout of the program. Teachers are accustomed to teaching a skill or concept to mastery. In *Everyday Mathematics,* skills and concepts are taught to mastery, but not necessarily upon the first presentation. Until teachers have some experience with the program, they typically will be uneasy with this cyclical approach.

This makes for great professional discussions among those teaching the program. However, this is not appropriate for sharing with parents. Would you feel comfortable leaving your child with a professional who voices concerns about whether what they are doing is in the best interest of your child?

Do not leave this to chance. Discuss communicating with parents on a regular basis—at staff meetings or training sessions. *Everyday Mathematics* is fun, and students will achieve well. Share your enthusiasm for and confidence in the program, and accept the responsibility for learning as much about the program as possible.

Communication must be proactive, planned, and purposeful—something we are traditionally not very good at in education. However, even given the time constraints and, for most of us, lack of formal training of this type, it is worth taking the time to be proactive. It is more enjoyable (and will result in overall time savings) to educate others about the program early on rather than defending the program later.

How do you decide upon the important communication points? Try this. If you were quoted in the newspaper, what key points would you communicate? If you had an opportunity in a meeting, in the grocery store, or in some other social situation to provide information about the program, what would you share? If you have a handful of points memorized, it is easy to insert them into both formal and informal interactions. Do not be shy about promoting the program. The up-front work will pay off in support and benefit for the students, parents, and teachers.

Keep in mind that adults have varied learning styles just as students do. Plan to address as many learning styles as possible. The program materials offer many suggestions and tools for varying the ways in which we communicate. Some parents will prefer information in newsletters, others will need to experience the hands-on activities, and still others will be interested in the research or real-life examples of successes in nearby communities.

The program materials have been around long enough that they are used in many districts. Find a

Do not be shy about promoting the program. The up-front work will pay off in support and benefit for the students, parents, and teachers.

nearby school, and talk to the teachers and administrators about their experiences. I found a district that actually had to create algebra classes for sixth-grade students because they were advanced enough to begin algebra at that point! What a great success story to share!

As any good public relations person will tell you, communicating once is not enough! Repetition of key points will reinforce learning. With Home Links and Study Links, make sure students are able to explain the problems to their parents and can complete the work independently. With a new program, parents are likely to feel unable to help their child with homework. In this way, the child is walking the parent through the homework as it is completed.

Write about math regularly in teacher and school newsletters. Both teachers and principals should be involved with the communications. Classroom newsletters written by students are an excellent way to get parents to read about math. Asking students for their comments about math lessons and quoting them in a newsletter always attracts readers.

Some of your best advocates will be parents who work in classrooms during the math periods. Get them in, and put them to work—and be sure to acknowledge their visits to the classroom in your newsletters!

Anticipate hot spots, and address them up front. If calculator use in primary grades is controversial, do not avoid the topic; instead, be proactive and confront it. Basic fact learning is typically another hot spot. Again, remember where parents are coming from, and remember the questions you had when first learning about the program.

Give parents an opportunity to learn by doing. In one school, I observed a Math Night where parents rotated through instructional groups. One of the groups focused on teaching algorithms. What a great way to help parents understand classroom instruction! In another school, the students led groups and instructed parents on classroom activities. In addition to providing parents with an understanding of the program, it ensures complete understanding on the part of the students.

Parents and educators have a common interest in wanting the best for students. Start from this common interest, and work with parents to understand why *Everyday Mathematics* is the best program for children. Not only will you create a larger pool of key communicators, but with greater parent understanding, you will increase the success of students!

*S*pecial Education and Everyday Mathematics

"Wow, a special education curriculum for the general education population!" As a parent of a child with special needs and as a teacher of *Everyday Mathematics,* that was my first reaction to this program. Special education has historically provided children with a custom-fit education, while the general education population received a one-size-fits-all approach. Teaching *Everyday Mathematics* in a full-inclusion classroom gave me the flexibility to meet all the students' needs with one best-practices program.

Teachers and parents look to you for reassurance and for a sound plan for meeting each child's unique needs. Your communications with them will be more frequent. Consistent with the philosophy of *Everyday Mathematics* that all children learn at their own pace and range, let parents know that this program is designed in its flexibility and with its separate components to meet the needs of all children.

Can My Child Attend Regular Classes?

It is important to understand the working philosophy of *Everyday Mathematics.* Inclusion in the regular instruction of *Everyday Mathematics* provides immersion in mathematical literacy. The content strand spiral provides all students with the exposures needed for learning specific skills at varying points in time. When possible, allowing students with special needs to benefit from the direct instruction portion of each lesson provided for the whole class at their appropriate grade level provides the language and experiences prerequisite to learning. You can make modifications and communicate them to the general education teacher. These could involve including the special education student for a portion of the lesson, varying from 15 to 20 minutes in the primary grades to 30 minutes in the intermediate grades.

When inclusion is not an option, you might compact the curriculum to provide key lessons in the spiral as they address a student's IEP objectives. Another approach is to use special education students as

Peg Rangel

Peg has taught grades 1–5 and special education in self-contained settings from primary through secondary. Her involvement with Everyday Mathematics *began in 1990 when she was one of the first to field-test the program. She has had the opportunity to collaborate on a U.S. Department of Education-funded project for students with learning disabilities that investigated different approaches to mathematical instruction and developed specific interventions in a full-inclusion setting.*

*T*eaching Everyday Mathematics *in a full-inclusion classroom gave me the flexibility to meet all the students' needs with one best-practices program.*

cross-age tutors. Being placed in lower grades as guides to younger children gives them both direct instruction at their appropriate academic levels as well as the shared language experience. Tutoring has added value as students receive recognition as teachers of others.

What Interventions Have You Provided My Child?

Provide a clear picture of what modifications to the *Everyday Mathematics* program you want to implement to remediate essential skills. Include in a student's IEP goals adaptations consistent with his or her abilities: abbreviate the journal pages, model and assist in completion of the pages, or omit the pages. While the rest of the class is working on the journal pages, redirect the student to an exploration or a game that specifically targets his or her needs. Then reverse the activities, using class game and exploration time to reteach or introduce remedial strategies to the special education pupil. The games and explorations are also wonderful opportunities for students to share their thinking and strategies.

It is highly effective to keep fluidity in your groupings of children, allowing much modeling and verbalizing. At times, you may want homogenous groups to focus on a specific skill. However, be sure to offer opportunities for heterogeneous groups to work together.

Math Boxes are easy to modify for independent seat work. With children functioning at a low academic level, Math Boxes can provide the bridge from concrete to pictorial and symbolic. Children can create cells and then make up number models and number families using dominoes and dice. Clipping the Math Boxes by cells and sorting them by concept can provide quick and easy access to the many paper-and-pencil devices *Everyday Mathematics* uses to reinforce counting and numeration skills. Remember, Math Boxes are a wonderful tool for sharing with parents the work children are doing on a daily basis. Math Boxes also provide parents with a clear representation of a child's performance versus grade-level expectations.

Will My Child Have the Tools Needed to Be a Problem-Solving Adult?

The greatest asset in using *Everyday Mathematics* is the systemic and consistent development of procedural thinking and algorithmic invention. There are many ways to solve a problem and many ways to provide compensatory skills. Tell parents we teach the child process rather than having the process done for the child. What good is a calculator if the child doesn't know when or why to use it? Tell your parents that throughout the program, the student is taught to ask the question "What am I looking for?" Encourage parents to elicit that question when helping with homework. Show them how to have the child collect, organize, and randomly generate data needed to answer the question. Demonstrate for parents specifically taught strategies and methods for solving problems.

All children learn well when concepts are taught in everyday, playful ways. The multiple components of *Everyday Mathematics* facilitate instruction in the general education classroom while targeting specific IEP objectives.

Teaching Mathematics in the Linguistically Diverse Classroom

Understanding the Needs of Children Acquiring English Proficiency

Regardless of their first language, children who are acquiring proficiency in English are faced with many of the same issues in the content classroom. These children are often from homes where a language other than English is used, and like all children of their age, they are fully language-capable in their home language. In their home language, they are able to ask questions, assert knowledge, communicate and understand new concepts and ideas, and ask for clarification when they do not understand. In short, they are able to perform all the language functions of their age group *in their home language.* However, in the English-speaking classroom, these children find themselves at a disadvantage. Their lack of English language skills is sometimes mistaken for a lack of cognitive abilities. They are sometimes equated with children who have learning disabilities. You will find that the children in your classroom who are in this transitional stage of achieving proficiency in English share some tendencies.

- They are reluctant to participate in whole-class discussions or to ask and answer questions.
- They have difficulty following oral and written instructions.
- They appear shy, withdrawn, or unmotivated.
- They have difficulty finishing in-class assignments and homework.

In most cases, the tendencies listed above are a result of a lack of proficiency in English. They are not an indication of behavioral or cognitive problems. Also remember that unlike children whose home and school languages are the same, children growing up in non-English-speaking households are further disadvantaged because they may not be able to receive reinforcement and assistance at home.

To engage children in the learning process and to help them master concepts, content must be made accessible. Following are strategies that can help students overcome some of the linguistic barriers to learning mathematics.

Dr. Shahrzad Mahootian

Shahrzad received her Ph.D. in linguistics from Northwestern University. Her areas of specialization are bilingualism, codeswitching, and language acquisiton. During her career, she has spent at least 15 years in various K–12 classrooms and served as the ESL consultant for the Elgin, Illinois, school district. Shahrzad is currently Chair of the Departments of Linguistics, Anthropology, and Philosophy at Northeastern Illinois University in Chicago.

... lack of English language skills is sometimes mistaken for a lack of cognitive abilities.

... remember that unlike children whose home and school languages are the same, children growing up in non-English-speaking households are further disadvantaged because they may not be able to receive reinforcement and assistance at home.

Strategies for Making Mathematics Accessible

➤ Create a nonthreatening environment for participation. Children should be given opportunities and encouraged, but not forced, to participate. For example, they should not be the first to be called on for answers. Instead, after establishing a question-answer pattern, you might ask the child if he or she wants to try the next question. Do not be discouraged if the child says no or keeps silent. Continue to provide other opportunities for participation, especially where the child can *show* rather than provide a verbal response. It is also important to provide children with positive feedback. Let them know when they are right or on the right track. Focus on the content of the response, and resist correcting grammatical errors in front of the whole class. A helpful technique that provides positive feedback and models correct usage is to repeat the child's answer using correct English. "That's right, $\frac{4}{8}$ is greater than $\frac{5}{12}$."

➤ Involve in group work. During small-group activities, it is important to mix the less proficient children with native English speakers. Mixed groups allow children to express ideas and to ask questions in a low-risk environment. The groups also allow children opportunities to go beyond language barriers and cultural differences and to get to know each other. Finally, teachers can use the small group activity time to monitor students more closely and give input and assistance with less risk of embarrassing the child.

➤ Introduce specialized vocabulary. Introduce new vocabulary by writing the word on the board accompanied with an example. Whenever you use the new term, point to it on the board for reinforcement. Words with multiple meanings can be especially problematic. For example, words such as *table* and *quarter,* can cause confusion for nonproficient children and steer their attention away from the lesson. It is best to introduce these words along with their multiple meanings. To help students distinguish between multiple meanings, use visual aids as often as possible.

➤ Provide visual cues. Whenever possible, provide visual input along with oral input. For example, write important or new information on the board, point to objects as you refer to them, and most importantly show students what you want them to do by modeling the task. Modeling is especially effective in small groups. It is often helpful to repeat the activity and then have children try it to determine whether they really understand.

➤ Clarify directions. It is often necessary to clarify directions for in-class and homework assignments. First, read the directions aloud with the students. Next, work through an example to show what needs to be done step-by-step. Number stories or problem-solving activities can be especially difficult. Whenever possible, assist students by reading through the problems with them. Remember that children who are acquiring English must unravel the language of the problem before they can set out to solve the problem.

Everyday Mathematics
Program Content

Many essays in the first part of this *Home Connection Handbook* make strong cases for communicating about math and about *Everyday Mathematics* with parents and other members of the community. The second part of this book contains materials to help you do just that.

Much of the information you will find here is already available in your *Teachers Resource Manuals* or *Teachers Lesson Guide.* But most parents don't have access to those materials. These pages are resources you can share with your parents on a schoolwide or a classroomwide basis. Copy some or all of the pages to distribute at meetings or at the beginning of the school year. Share the pages with families of students new to the program. In general, use the pages to help parents become better *Everyday Mathematics* partners.

Everyday Mathematics
Program Components

Everyday Mathematics is a rich and varied program that enables elementary students to learn more mathematical content and become life-long mathematical thinkers. This second edition of the program integrates ongoing project research and the experiences and recommendations of teachers.

Teacher Materials

The *Everyday Mathematics* program provides a cohesive and balanced curriculum for grades K–6. These materials were developed by the University of Chicago School Mathematics Project (UCSMP) author team, reviewed by mathematics professionals, and tested in classrooms across the country. Because your child's school and teachers are using these teaching materials, your child benefits from the expertise of researchers, mathematics educators, and classroom teachers from around the country.

Student Materials
Student Reference Book (Grades 3–6)
Students use this book to find information and procedures that support their math lessons. This

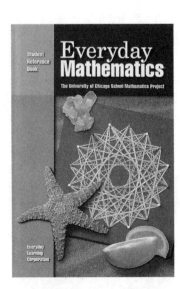

book contains information arranged by topic, such as game rules, ongoing routines, reference tables, a glossary of terms, and calculator usage.

Student Math Journal, Volumes 1 and 2 (Grades 1–6)
These consumable books contain materials that allow students to record, demonstrate, and practice what they are learning. The Math Journal becomes a long-term record of your child's mathematical development.

Everyday Mathematics
Features

Daily Routines

A routine is a familiar set of steps we follow to reach a goal. A routine allows us to focus on the results of the steps without being distracted by the steps themselves. For children, routines allow them to feel secure and to confidently anticipate events in a day.

Routines at home can help children make connections between their everyday lives and their school work. Most classrooms have daily routines, such as taking attendance and tracking the date or the weather. In the *Everyday Mathematics* classroom, children take an active role in these routines. As a result, children gain valuable experience in both taking responsibility and connecting mathematics to everyday activities.

Routines in the *Everyday Mathematics* Program

Just as daily routines at home and in the classroom offer rich opportunities for children to practice math skills, *Everyday Mathematics* program routines encourage ongoing practice in a number of mathematics skills and content areas. Most of the routines in *Everyday Mathematics* are introduced in the first unit. Afterward, they become self-sustaining, as much by the children's energy as by the teacher's effort.

Some of the routines children learn and work with regularly are these:

- Mental Math and Reflexes
- Math Message
- Home Links
- Name-Collection Boxes
- Math Boxes
- Frames and Arrows
- Fact Triangles
- What's My Rule?

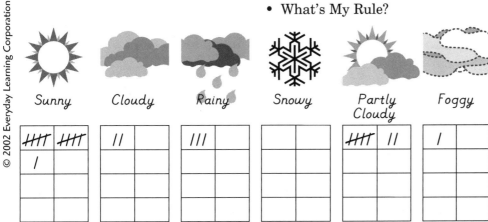

Your child can use tally marks and symbols to keep track of the weather. He or she can use the information to make decisions about how to dress for the day. Gathering data is an important math skill. The data can be graphed and compared.

Walking Through a Lesson

Getting Started

Each lesson in *Everyday Mathematics* includes a section called "Getting Started." This section always contains a quick mental math activity called Mental Math and Reflexes and a Math Message activity. These routines provide a lesson and "warm up" and help prepare the children for the lesson's learning objectives.

Mental Math and Reflexes

The term *Mental Math and Reflexes* refers to exercises, usually oral, designed to strengthen children's number sense and to review and advance essential basic skills. Mental Math and Reflexes sessions usually last no longer than five minutes. For this type of activity, numerous short interactions are more effective than fewer prolonged sessions.

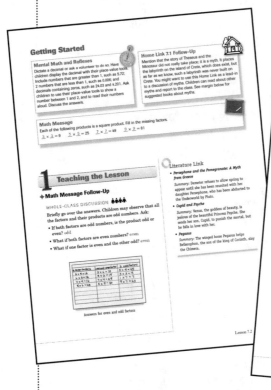

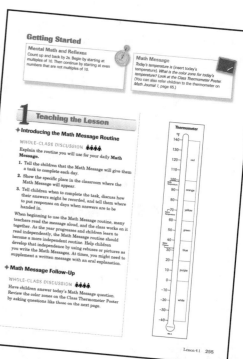

© 2002 Everyday Learning Corporation

There are several kinds of Mental Math activities. Some involve a choral counting routine; many are basic-skills practice with counts, operations, and measures; some are problem-solving exercises.

Math Message

A Math Message is provided at the beginning of each lesson beginning with Unit 4 in first grade. The Math Message usually leads into the lesson for the day, including occasional reviews of topics previously covered. Children complete the Math Message before the start of each lesson.

The teacher might display the Math Message in a number of ways. The Math Message might be written on the board, on an oversized pad of paper, or on an overhead transparency. Some teachers have children record their answers to the Math Message. Answers could be recorded in the Math Journals, or teachers might record answers on half sheets of paper, which they collect from time to time.

Teachers often use Math Messages in *Everyday Mathematics* as guides to developing their own activities, which they can design specifically for the needs of the children in their classroom.

Home Link

Home Links are the *Everyday Mathematics* version of homework assignments. Each lesson has a Home Link. During the "Getting Started" section, the previous Home Link is reviewed, so it is important for your child to bring the Home Link back to school completed each day. Home Links consist of active projects and ongoing review problems and serve three main purposes: (1) They promote follow-up, (2) they provide enrichment, and (3) they offer an opportunity for you to become involved in your child's mathematics education. Many Home Links require children to interact with you or someone else at home.

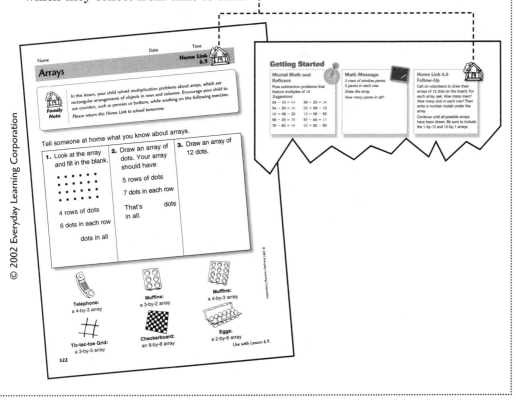

Parts of a Lesson

Each lesson in *Everyday Mathematics* follows a three-part plan: Part 1, Teaching the Lesson; Part 2, Ongoing Learning and Practice; and Part 3, Options for Individualizing.

Part 1: Teaching the Lesson

The main part of every lesson, Teaching the Lesson, is where the main instructional activities are found. Within these activities, most of the new content is introduced.

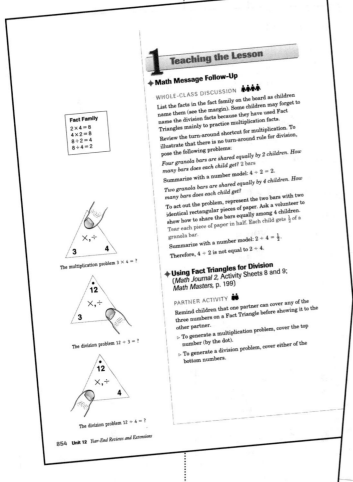

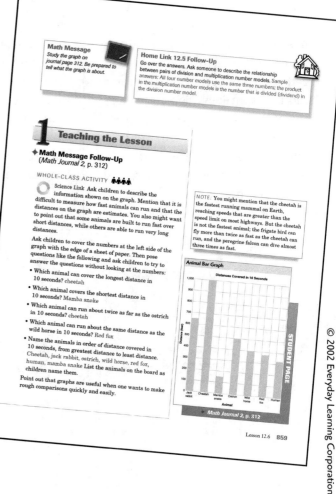

Part 2: Ongoing Learning and Practice

In the Ongoing Learning and Practice part of every lesson, students develop and maintain skills. These activities provide opportunities for students to develop concepts and skills recently introduced, and review and practice familiar content. Activities may involve Math Journal Assignments, Math Boxes, Home Links, Study Links, and games.

Games

Frequent practice is necessary for children to build, master, and maintain strong mental-arithmetic skills and reflexes. Although drills have their place, most of the practice in *Everyday Mathematics* is in the form of games. Games are an enjoyable way to practice number skills, and since children enjoy them so much, they often want to continue to play math games during their free time. This means students are practicing mathematics skills more than they ordinarily would if they used only drills.

The games are fun to do, but mathematics skills are needed to play them. The game format eliminates the tedium of most drills, so children will want to stay involved. A balance between drills and games is the best approach.

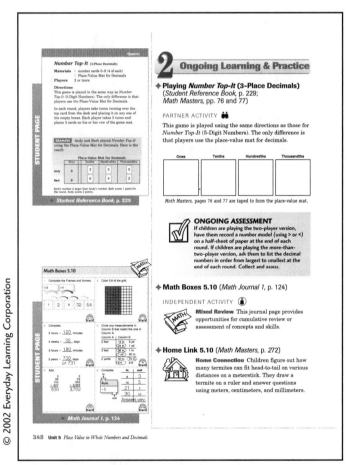

In this lesson, students are introduced to thousandths by using millimeters and to interpreting weather data from a map. Many *Everyday Mathematics* lessons integrate other school subjects, such as social studies, science, and reading.

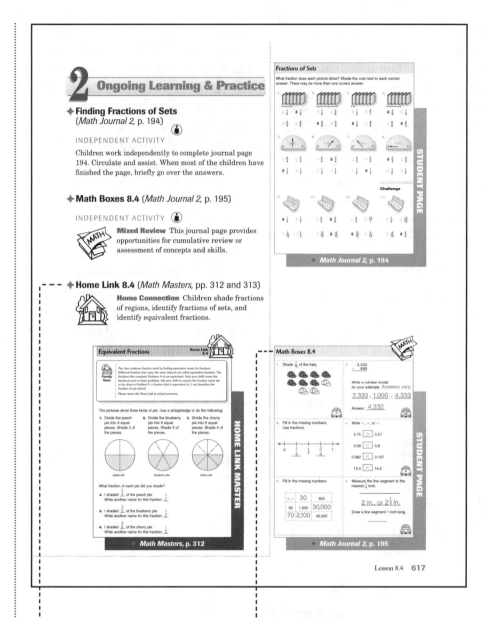

Math Journal 2, p. 194

Math Masters, p. 312

Math Journal 2, p. 195

Lesson 8.4   **617**

Home Link

Home Links are the *Everyday Mathematics* version of homework assignments. Each lesson has a Home Link. A summary of the lesson is included in the Home Link. During the "Getting Started" section, the previous Home Link is reviewed.

Math Boxes

Math Boxes were originally developed by an *Everyday Mathematics* teacher. They are excellent for ongoing practice and maintenance. Math Boxes provide continuous practice of all skills and concepts in the program. Math Boxes are designed as independent activities. Some teacher involvement may be necessary, especially at the beginning of the school year. With Math Boxes, lesson activities are revisited throughout the school year. Math Boxes might also be used to assess skills.

Part 3: Options for Individualizing

The third part of each lesson is called Options for Individualizing. It provides extra opportunities for meeting the needs of different types of students. Reteaching activities provide additional instructional support for concepts presented in the lesson. Enrichment activities provide suggestions for extending the lesson. Extra Practice gives students opportunities to work more with the ideas in the lesson. Other suggestions in this part of the lesson include individual or small-group activities and language diversity features that support children acquiring proficiency in English.

---

3 Options for Individualizing

✦ EXTRA PRACTICE Creating Alternative Place-Value Tools (*Math Masters*, pp. 85–91)

SMALL-GROUP ACTIVITY 👥👥👥👥 15–30 min

Below are alternatives to the place-value flip book. If you prefer, you can have children make one of these.

Compact Place-Value Flip Book
(*Math Masters*, pp. 85–88)

1. Cut each page along the dotted lines. Do NOT cut any of the solid lines.
2. Cut along the vertical dotted lines to separate the digits on each page.
3. Assemble the pages in order.
4. Staple the assembled book. (Children may need a little help with this step.)

Plastic-Wrap-Box Card Holder
(*Math Masters*, pp. 89 and 90)

1. Remove the metal strip from a plastic wrap or similar box. (This step should be done by an adult—you or a parent.)
2. Fold the lid into the box so that digit cards can sit in the space between the lid and the box.
3. Paper clip place-value labels (tens, ones, tenths, hundredths, and thousandths or ten-thousands, thousands, hundreds, tens, and ones) onto the front of the box. Be sure that the labels are evenly spaced. Note that a decimal point is included at the right side of the "ones" label.

Paper Card-Holder
(*Math Masters*, pp. 90 and 91)

1. Fold along the dashed line on *Math Masters*, page 91.
2. Staple on the heavy lines between the places to make small pockets to hold the digit cards.

Paper Card-Holder

NOTE: The Compact Place-Value Flip Book can be used to display numbers from 99,999 to 0.0001. To use the book for decimals, fold back the place-value labels. On the last page in each place where there are decimal points, so a wide range of mixed numbers can be displayed.

Compact Place-Value Flip Book

NOTE: Depending on the place-value labels chosen, the Plastic-Wrap-Box Card Holder can display numbers from 99,999 to 0.001. *Math Masters*, page 90 contains one each of the digits 0–9. Make multiple copies of the master for more copies of each digit.

Plastic-Wrap-Box Card Holder
(Digit cards are on *Math Masters*, page 90 and place-value labels are on *Math Masters*, page 89.)

NOTE: The Paper Card-Holder can be used to display numbers from 99.999 to 0.001. *Math Masters*, page 90 contains one copy of each of the digits 0–9. Make multiple copies of the master for more copies of each digit.

---

3 Options for Individualizing

✦ ENRICHMENT Polygons in Literature

WHOLE-CLASS ACTIVITY 👥👥👥👥 5–15 min

Literature Link *The Greedy Triangle* by Marilyn Burns (Scholastic, 1994) focuses on the characteristics of different polygons. A triangle, dissatisfied with its life, goes to the Shapeshifter and asks for one more angle and one more side. Life as a square is then explored. The story continues in this manner as the shape continually asks the Shapeshifter for one more angle and one more side. Eventually the shape returns to being a triangle.

✦ ENRICHMENT Solving a Polygon Cut-up Problem (*Math Masters*, p. 97)

SMALL-GROUP ACTIVITY 👥👥👥👥 5–15 min

Children cut out the rectangle and the parallelogram on *Math Masters*, page 97 and then cut each shape into pieces along the dashed lines. Then they rearrange the pieces of the rectangle to form a square and the pieces of the parallelogram to form another square. The pieces should not overlap. Then children glue or tape the squares onto a sheet of paper and label each solution with the name of the polygon with which they started.

Have children compare solutions. Ask: *Is there more than one way to arrange the pieces of a given polygon into a square?* no *Do the two squares have the same area?* yes

✦ RETEACHING Performing Polygon Calisthenics

SMALL-GROUP ACTIVITY 👥👥👥👥 5–15 min

Use a loop of light rope or heavy cord to further demonstrate the variety of possible polygons. Start with 5 children as vertices, and then add more vertices.

The following ideas might be discussed:

▷ Since the loop length remains constant, some sides get shorter as more vertices are added.
▷ More vertices mean larger angles.
▷ As more vertices are added to a regular polygon, the polygon becomes more and more like a circle.

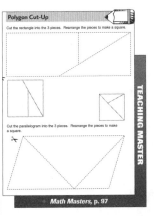

Polygon Cut-Up

Cut the rectangle into the 3 pieces. Rearrange the pieces to make a square.

Cut the parallelogram into the 3 pieces. Rearrange the pieces to make a square.

TEACHING MASTER

Math Masters, p. 97

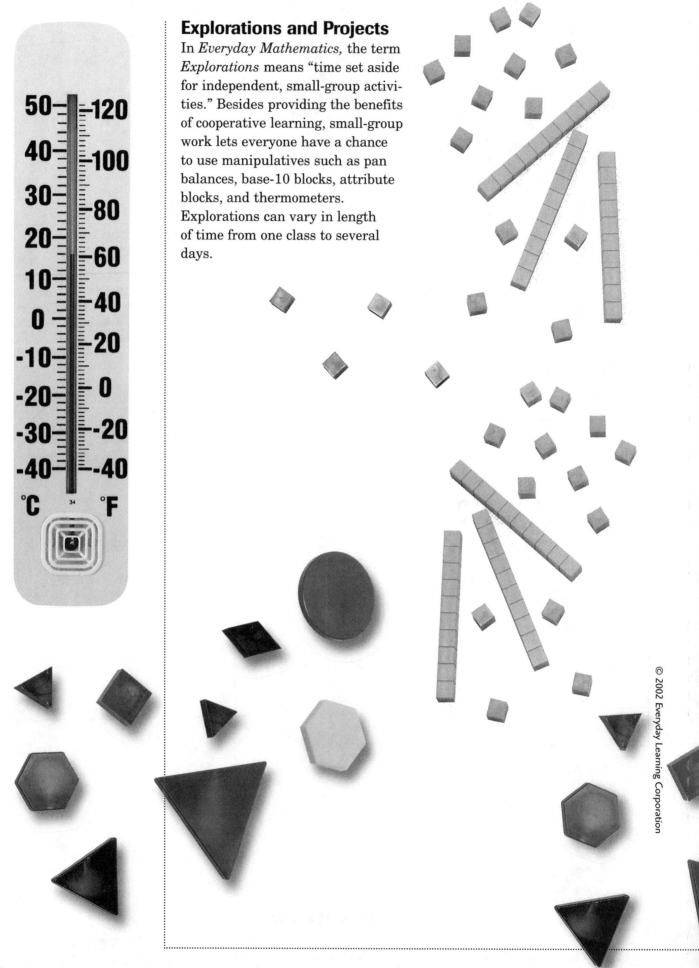

Explorations and Projects

In *Everyday Mathematics,* the term *Explorations* means "time set aside for independent, small-group activities." Besides providing the benefits of cooperative learning, small-group work lets everyone have a chance to use manipulatives such as pan balances, base-10 blocks, attribute blocks, and thermometers. Explorations can vary in length of time from one class to several days.

Name-Collection Boxes

Beginning in first grade, children use name-collection boxes to help manage equivalent names for numbers. These devices offer a simple way for children to experience the notion that numbers can be expressed many different ways. Names for the same number can include sums, differences, products, quotients, the results of combining several operations, words in English or other languages, tally marks, arrays, Roman numerals, and so on.

In kindergarten through third grade, a name-collection box is a diagram of a box with a label attached to it. The name on the label identifies the number whose names are inside the box. For example, the boxes on this page show a 16-box, a 25-box, and a 14-box.

Beginning in fourth grade, *Everyday Mathematics* introduces a simpler and more compact name-collection box like the one on the right.

14
1,400%
2 * 7
20 − 6
1 + 13
700/50
$3^3 - 13$
0.028 * 500
XIV
(3 * 7) − 7

16	XVI
	10 less than 26
20 − 4	
	4 + 4 + 4 + 4
(2 × 5) + 6	dieciséis
	sixteen
half of 32	116 − 100
	8 twos
	32 ÷ 2

10 + 2 − 4 + 6 − 8 + 10

25	37 − 12	20 + 5

||||| ||||| ||||| ||||| |||||

twenty-five

veinticinco

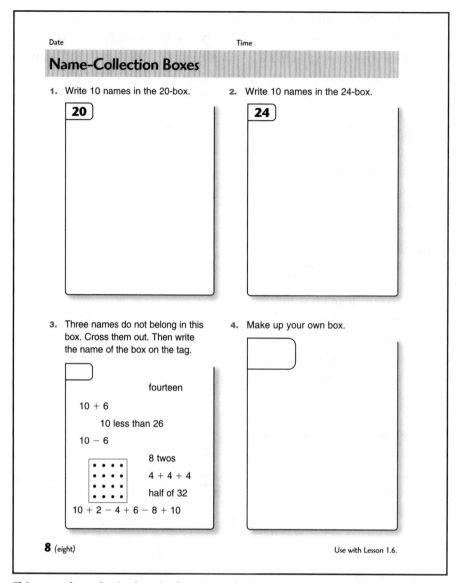

Name-Collection Boxes

1. Write 10 names in the 20-box.

20

2. Write 10 names in the 24-box.

24

3. Three names do not belong in this box. Cross them out. Then write the name of the box on the tag.

fourteen

10 + 6

10 less than 26

10 − 6

8 twos

4 + 4 + 4

half of 32

10 + 2 − 4 + 6 − 8 + 10

4. Make up your own box.

8 (eight)

Use with Lesson 1.6.

This page, from the Grade 3 *Student Journal,* shows four variations on using Name-Collection Boxes. When the teacher brings children together to discuss the activity, they enjoy sharing names no one else thought of! Try Problem 4 with your child. Then talk about the variety of names you and your child wrote in the box.

Frames and Arrows

Frames-and-Arrows diagrams provide children with a way to organize work with sequences. They are made up of shapes, called frames, connected by arrows to show the path for moving from one frame to another. Each frame contains a number in the sequence. Each arrow represents the rule that tells what number goes in the next frame. Frames-and-Arrows diagrams are also called chains. Here is a simple example of a Frames-and-Arrows diagram for the rule "Add 1."

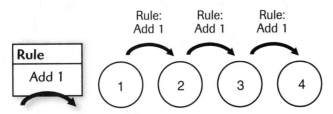

In Frames-and-Arrows problems, some information is missing. Here are several examples:

1. The rule is given. Some of the frames are empty. Fill in the blank frames.

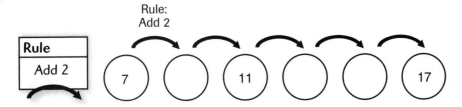

Solution: Write 9, 13, and 15 in the blank frames.

2. The frames are filled in. The rule is missing. Find the rule.

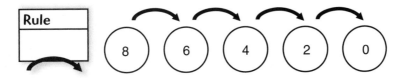

Solution: The rule is subtract 2, minus 2, or −2.

3. Some of the frames are empty. The rule is missing. Find the rule, and fill in the empty frames.

Solution: The rule is add 1. Write 8 and 11 in the empty frames.

A chain can have more than one arrow rule. If it does, the arrows for the rules must look different. For example, we can use a black arrow for one rule and a gray arrow for the other rule:

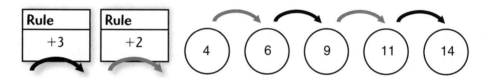

In the following example, the rules and frames are given, but the arrows are missing:

4. Draw the arrows in the proper positions.

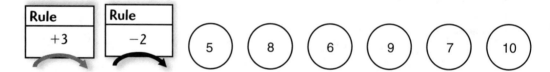

Solution: Draw the + 3 arrow from 5 to 8, from 6 to 9, and from 7 to 10. Draw the –2 arrow from 8 to 6 and from 9 to 7.

What's My Rule?

"What's My Rule?" is an activity in which children analyze a set of number pairs to determine the rule that relates the numbers in each pair. Simple "What's My Rule?" games begin in kindergarten *Everyday Mathematics*. The first are attribute rules or activities that sort children into a specified group. For example, children with laces on their shoes belong, while children whose shoes don't have laces don't belong.

In first through third grades, this idea is extended to include numbers and rules for determining which numbers belong to specific sets of numbers. For example, the teacher might draw a circle on the board and begin writing numbers inside and outside the circle. The children suggest numbers and try to guess where they go. Once they can predict reliably which number belongs inside the circle, they propose rules for the sorting.

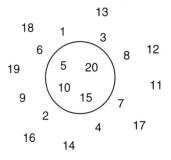

This idea evolves further to incorporate sets of number pairs in which the numbers in each pair are related to each other according to the same rule. The connections between input, output, and the rule can be represented by a function machine, and pairings are displayed in a table of values.

In a "What's My Rule?" problem, two of the three parts—input, output, and rule—are known. The goal is to find the unknown part.

There are three types of "What's My Rule?" problems.

1. The rule and the input numbers are known. Find the output numbers.

Rule: +10	
In	Out
39	
54	
163	

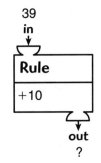

2. The rule and the output numbers are known. Find the input numbers.

Rule: −6	
In	Out
	6
	10
	20

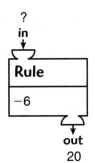

3. The input and output numbers
are known. Find the rule.

Rule: ?	
In	Out
55	60
85	90
103	108

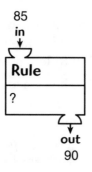

85
in

Rule

?

out
90

You can combine more than one
type of problem in a single table.
For instance, you could give the
table in Problem 2 but give the
input value of 26 and replace the
20 with a blank. If you give enough
input and output clues, children
can fill in the blanks as well as figure out the rule, as in the problem
below.

Rule: ?	
In	Out
	6
	10
26	

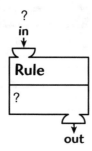

?
in

Rule

?

out

Fact Power

"Knowing" the basic number facts is as important to learning mathematics as "knowing" words by sight is to reading. Students are often told that habits—good and bad—come from doing something over and over until they do it without thinking. Developing basic number-fact reflexes can be likened to developing good habits.

In *Everyday Mathematics,* fact habits are referred to as *fact power.* Children in Grades 1–3 keep Fact Power tables of the facts they know. By the end of second grade most children should master the addition and subtraction facts. In third grade, the emphasis shifts to learning the multiplication and division facts. While some students may not be able to demonstrate mastery of all these facts, they should be well on their way to achieving this goal by the end of the year.

Practicing the facts is often tedious and traditionally involves many pages filled with drill-and-practice problems. In addition to number games and choral drills (short drills often written on the board that review facts), teachers of *Everyday Mathematics* have had success with fact families.

Facts Table

+,−	0	1	2	3	4	5	6	7	8	9
0	0	1	2	3	4	5	6	7	8	9
1	1	2	3	4	5	6	7	8	9	10
2	2	3	4	5	6	7	8	9	10	11
3	3	4	5	6	7	8	9	10	11	12
4	4	5	6	7	8	9	10	11	12	13
5	5	6	7	8	9	10	11	12	13	14
6	6	7	8	9	10	11	12	13	14	15
7	7	8	9	10	11	12	13	14	15	16
8	8	9	10	11	12	13	14	15	16	17
9	9	10	11	12	13	14	15	16	17	18

Fact Families

Everyday Mathematics research has found that young children not only can understand the inverse relationships between arithmetic operations (addition "undoes" subtraction and vice versa; multiplication "undoes" division and vice versa), they often "discover" them on their own. In first- and second-grade *Everyday Mathematics,* the inverses for sums and differences of whole numbers up to 10 are called the basic fact families. A fact family is a collection of four related facts linking two inverse operations. For example, the following four equations symbolize the fact family relating 3, 4, and 7 with addition and subtraction:

$$3 + 4 = 7 \qquad 4 + 3 = 7$$
$$7 - 3 = 4 \qquad 7 - 4 = 3$$

Basic fact families are modeled with Fact Triangles.

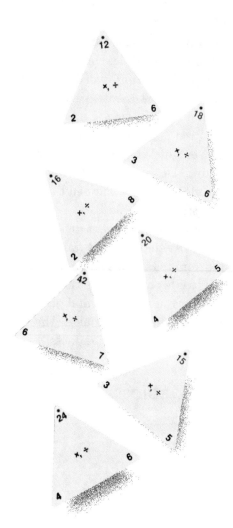

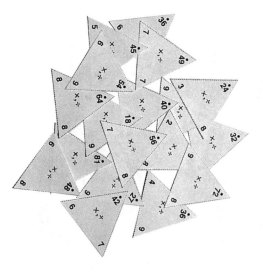

Fact Triangles

Fact Triangles are tools used to help build mental arithmetic reflexes. You might think of them as the *Everyday Mathematics* version of flash cards. Fact Triangles are more effective for helping children memorize facts, however, because of their emphasis on fact families.

In first grade, children play with Fact Triangles for addition/subtraction fact families through $9 + 9$ and $18 - 9$. These families are reviewed in second grade, and multiplication/division Fact Triangles are introduced. In third grade, children get addition/subtraction and multiplication/division Fact Triangles. In all grades, a useful long-term project is to have students write the appropriate four number models on the back of each Fact Triangle.

Fact Triangles are best used with partners. One player covers a corner with a finger, and the other player gives an addition or subtraction (or multiplication or division) fact that has the hidden number as an answer. This simple game makes it easy for children to play at home, so Fact Triangles are often recommended in Home Links.

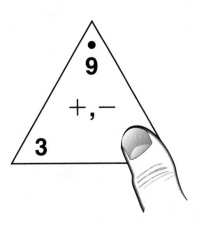

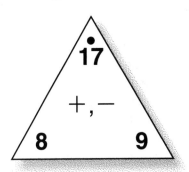

Addition/Subtraction Fact Triangle

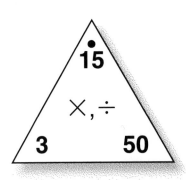

Multiplication/Division Fact Triangle

Slates

Slates are used often, especially in the Mental Math and Reflexes—a brief five-minute activity that begins each lesson. Slate use provides a quick way to check children's work as they respond to questions and then display their answers on their slates. Most children genuinely enjoy using slates. Slates allow everyone to quietly answer a question at the same time, and they help the teacher see at a glance which children may need extra help. They also save paper!

Calculators

Both teacher experience and educational research show that most children can develop good judgment about when to use and when not to use calculators. Students need to learn how to decide when it is appropriate to solve an arithmetic problem by estimating or calculating mentally, by using paper and pencil, or by using a calculator. The evidence indicates that children who use calculators are able to choose appropriately.

Calculators are useful teaching tools. They make it possible for young children to display numbers before they are skilled at writing. Calculators can be used to count forward or backward by any whole number or decimal—a particularly important activity in the primary grades because counting is so central to number and operations at this level. Calculators also allow children to solve interesting everyday problems requiring computations that might otherwise be too difficult for them to perform, including problems that arise outside of mathematics class. There is no evidence to suggest that this will cause children to become dependent on calculators or make them unable to solve problems mentally or with paper and pencil.

Before the availability of inexpensive calculators, the elementary school mathematics curriculum was designed primarily so that children would become skilled at carrying out algorithms. Thus there was little time left for children to learn to think mathematically and solve problems. Calculators enable children to think about the problems themselves, rather than thinking only about carrying out algorithms without mistakes.

Talk to your child's teacher about the use of calculators in his or her classroom. Your child's teacher can also give you suggestions for further reading from the *Teacher's Reference Manual* about research done on the use of calculators by children.

Beat the Calculator

A "Calculator" (a player who uses a calculator to solve the problem) and a "Brain" (a player who solves the problem without a calculator) race to see who will be first to solve addition problems.

*I*ntroduction to Algorithms

Even if you've never heard the word *algorithm,* it is a part of the working vocabulary of your children when they use the *Everyday Mathematics* program. Algorithms are actually a working part of your everyday life. Have you ever had to follow the directions for assembling a new toy for your child's birthday? Do you use a recipe when making your favorite cookies? How about when you use a microwave? Isn't there a certain procedure you have to follow if you want to defrost something? Each of these examples illustrates the use of an algorithm. Here is the official definition: An algorithm is a well-defined procedure or set of rules guaranteed to achieve a certain objective.

Here's a mathematics example: An algorithm for multiplication is a specific series of steps that will give you the correct answer no matter what numbers you multiply together. You probably used one particular algorithm for multiplying when you were in grade school—and it was most likely the same algorithm that all your fellow classmates memorized too. No one knew why it worked, but it did! Your child is

learning that there is more than one algorithm for solving multiplication problems—or addition or subtraction or division problems. If children understand the mathematics behind the problem, they may very well be able to come up with a unique working algorithm that proves they "get it." Helping children become comfortable with algorithmic and procedural thinking is essential to their growth and development in mathematics and as everyday problem solvers.

Computation in Everyday Mathematics

The treatment of computation in *Everyday Mathematics* involves three stages:

- In the early phases of learning an operation, children are encouraged to invent their own procedures. They are asked to solve non-routine problems involving the operations before they have developed or learned systematic procedures for solving such problems. This approach requires students to focus on the meaning of the operation. It also provides a meaningful context for developing accurate and efficient procedures.
- Later, when students thoroughly understand the concept of the operation, they examine several alternative algorithms. In this stage, students are encouraged to experiment with various algorithms and to become proficient with at least one.
- Finally, students are asked to demonstrate proficiency in at least one method. The program offers a focus algorithm for each operation to facilitate and support this phase of instruction. All students are expected to demonstrate proficiency with the focus algorithms, though they are not required to use them if they have alternatives they prefer. Focus algorithms provide a common language for further work, especially across grade levels and classrooms, and offer reliable alternatives for children who have not developed effective procedures on their own.

Algorithm Invention

Everyday Mathematics believes that children should be encouraged to invent and share their own procedures. As children devise their own methods, they use prior mathematical knowledge and common sense, along with new skills and knowledge. They also learn that their intuitive methods are valid and that mathematics makes sense. Ideally, children should develop a variety of computational methods and the flexibility to choose the procedure that is most appropriate in a given situation.

It is important that children have a chance to develop their own computation methods *before* they receive formal instruction in algorithms, especially standard algorithms. Learning standard algorithms too early may inhibit the development of their mathematical understanding and cause them to miss the rich experiences that come from developing their own methods. *Extensive research shows the main problem with teaching standard algorithms too early is that children then use the algorithms as*

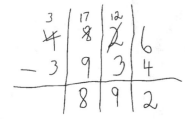

substitutes for thinking and common sense. For example, the authors of *Everyday Mathematics* presented the problem shown on the far right to a large number of children.

Most second and third graders immediately resorted to the standard algorithm, often failing to get the correct answer. Only a handful of children interpreted the problem as asking, "What number plus 1 gives 300?" or "What number is 1 less than 300?" or "What is the number just before 300?" and answered 299 without performing any computation.

In the modern world, most adults reach for calculators when faced with any moderately complex arithmetic computation. This behavior is sensible and should be an option for children too. Nevertheless, children do benefit in the following ways from developing their own noncalculator procedures:

- Children are more motivated when they don't have to learn standard paper-and-pencil algorithms by rote. People are more interested in what they can understand, and children generally understand their own methods.

- Children become adept at changing the representation of ideas and problems, translating readily among manipulatives, oral and written words, pictures, and symbols. The ability to represent a problem in more than one way is important in problem solving.

- Children develop the ability to transform a given problem into an equivalent, easier problem. For example, they recognize that $32 - 17$ can be transformed into $35 - 20$.

- In trying out creative problem-solving strategies, and in refining those strategies for use on a more permanent basis, children gain experience in decision making.

Alternative Algorithms

After children have had plenty of opportunities to experiment with their own computational strategies, they are introduced to several algorithms for each operation. Some of these algorithms may be identical to or closely resemble methods children devised on their own. Others are simplifications or modifications of traditional algorithms or wholly new algorithms that may have significant advantages to children and in today's technological world. Still others are traditional algorithms, including the standard algorithms customarily taught in U.S. classrooms.

Demonstrating Proficiency

Everyday Mathematics believes that children should be proficient with *at least* one algorithm for each operation. The program offers one *focus algorithm* for each operation to support this phase of children's mathematical development.

Students learn one focus algorithm for each operation. Focus algorithms are powerful, efficient, and easy to understand and learn. They also provide common and consistent language, terminology and support across grade levels of the curriculum. All children are expected to demonstrate proficiency with algorithms. Once they can reliably use the focus algorithm, children are encouraged to use it or any other method to solve problems. The aim of this approach is to promote flexibility and use of alternative methods while ensuring that all children know at least one reliable method for each operation.

$$300$$
$$-\ \ \ 1$$

Addition Algorithms

This section presents just a few of the dozens of possible algorithms for adding whole numbers.

Focus Algorithm: Partial-Sums

You can add two numbers by calculating partial-sums, working one place-value column at a time, and then adding all the sums to find the total.

Example: Partial Sums

	268
	+ 483
Add the hundreds (200 + 400).	600
Add the tens (60 + 80).	140
Add the ones (8 + 3).	+ 11
Add the partial sums (600 + 140 + 11).	751

Column-Addition

To add using the column-addition algorithm, draw vertical lines to separate the ones, tens, hundreds, and so on. Add the digits in each column, and then adjust the results.

Example: Column Addition

Add the digits in each column.

	hundreds	tens	ones
	2	6	8
+	4	8	3
	6	14	11

Since 14 tens is 1 hundred plus 4 tens, add 1 to the hundreds column, and change the number in the tens column to 4.

	hundreds	tens	ones
	2	6	8
+	4	8	3
	7	4	11

Since 11 ones is 1 ten plus 1 one, add 1 to the tens column, and change the number in the ones column to 1.

	hundreds	tens	ones
	2	6	8
+	4	8	3
	7	5	1

For some students, the above process becomes so automatic that they start at the left and write the answer column by column, adjusting as they go without writing any of the intermediate steps. If asked to explain, they might say something like this:

"200 plus 400 is 600. But (looking at the next column) I need to adjust that, so I write 7. 60 and 80 is 140. But that needs adjusting, so I write 5. 8 and 3 is 11. With no more to do, I can just write 1."

Opposite-Change Rule

If you add a number to one part of a sum and subtract the same number from the other part, the result remains the same. For example, consider:

$$8 + 7 = 15$$

Now add 2 to the 8, and subtract 2 from the 7:

$$(8 + 2) + (7 - 2) = 10 + 5 = 15$$

This idea can be used to rename the numbers being added so that one of them ends in zeros.

Example: Opposite Change

• Rename the first number and then the second.

Add 2.	Add 30.	
268	270	300
+ 483	+ 481	+ 451
Subtract 2.	Subtract 30.	751

• Rename the second number and then the first.

Subtract 7.	Subtract 10.	
268	261	251
+ 483	+ 490	+ 500
Add 7.	Add 10.	751

Subtraction Algorithms

There are even more algorithms for subtraction than for addition, probably because subtraction is more difficult. This section presents several subtraction algorithms.

Focus Algorithm: Trade-First Subtraction

This algorithm is similar to the traditional U.S. algorithm except that all the trading is done before the subtraction, allowing students to concentrate on one thing at a time.

Counting-Up

To subtract using the counting-up algorithm, start with the number you are subtracting (the subtrahend), and "count up" to the number you are subtracting from (the minuend) in stages. Keep track of the amounts you count up at each stage. When you are finished, find the sum of the amounts.

Example: Trade-First Subtraction

Examine the columns. You want to make trades so that the top number in each column is as large as or larger than the bottom number.

hundreds	tens	ones
9	3	2
− 3	5	6

To make the top number in the ones column larger than the bottom number, borrow 1 ten. The top number in the ones column becomes 12, and the top number in the tens column becomes 2.

hundreds	tens	ones
	2	12
9	$\cancel{3}$	$\cancel{2}$
− 3	5	6

To make the top number in the tens column larger than the bottom number, borrow 1 hundred. The top number in the tens column becomes 12, and the top number in the hundreds column becomes 8.

hundreds	tens	ones
	12	
8	$\cancel{2}$	12
$\cancel{9}$	$\cancel{3}$	$\cancel{2}$
− 3	5	6

Now subtract column by column in any order.

hundreds	tens	ones
	12	
8	$\cancel{2}$	12
$\cancel{9}$	$\cancel{3}$	$\cancel{2}$
− 3	5	6
5	7	6

Example: Counting Up

To find $932 - 356$, start with 356 and count up to 932.

356

360   Add 4 to count up to the nearest ten.

400   Add 40 to count up to the nearest hundred.

900   Add 500 to count up to the largest possible 100.

932   Add 32 to count up to 932.

Now find the sum of the numbers you added.

```
     4
    40
   500
 +  32
 ─────
   576
```

So, $932 - 356 = 576$.

Example: Left-to-Right Subtraction

To find $932 - 356$, think of 356 as the sum $300 + 50 + 6$. Then subtract the parts of the sum one at a time, starting from the hundreds.

	932
Subtract the hundreds.	$-$ 300
	632
Subtract the tens.	$-$ 50
	582
Subtract the ones.	$-$ 6
	576

Left-to-Right Subtraction

To use this algorithm, think of the number you are subtracting as a sum of ones, tens, hundreds, and so on. Then subtract one part of the sum at a time.

Example: Same-Change Rule

Add the same number.

Add 4.		Add 40.	
932	$\longrightarrow$	936	976
$-$ 356		$-$ 360	$-$ 400
		Subtract.	576

Example

Subtract the same number.

Subtract 6.		Subtract 50.	
932	$\longrightarrow$	926	876
$-$ 356		$-$ 350	$-$ 300
		Subtract.	576

The Same-Change Rule

If you add or subtract the same number from both parts of a subtraction problem, the results remain the same. Consider, for example:

$$15 - 8 = 7$$

Now add 4 to both the 15 and the 8:

$$(15 + 4) - (8 + 4) = 19 - 12 = 7$$

Or subtract 6 from both the 15 and the 8:

$$(15 - 6) - (8 - 6) = 9 - 2 = 7$$

The same-change algorithm uses this idea to rename both numbers so the number being subtracted ends in zeros.

Multiplication Algorithms

Children's experiences with addition and subtraction algorithms can help them invent multiplication algorithms. For example, when estimating a product mentally, many children begin to compute partial products: "Ten of these would be. . ., so 30 of them would be. . ., and we need 5 more, so. . ." Beginning in third-grade *Everyday Mathematics,* this approach is formalized as the partial-products multiplication algorithm. This algorithm and others are discussed in this section.

Focus Algorithm: Partial Products

To use the partial-products algorithm, think of each factor as the sum of ones, tens, hundreds, and so on. Then multiply each part of one sum by each part of the other, and add the results.

Rectangular arrays can be used to demonstrate visually how the partial-products algorithm works. The product 14×23 is the number of dots in a 14-by-23 array. The diagram below shows how each of the partial products is represented in the array.

Example: Partial Products

To find 67×53, think of 67 as $60 + 7$ and 53 as $50 + 3$. Then multiply each part of one sum by each part of the other, and add the results.

	67
	$\times$ 53
Calculate 50×60.	3,000
Calculate 50×7.	350
Calculate 3×60.	180
Calculate 3×7.	+ 21
Add the results.	3,551

$$14 \times 23 = (10 + 4) \times (20 + 3)$$
$$= (10 \times 20) + (10 \times 3) + (4 \times 20) + (4 \times 3)$$
$$= 200 + 30 + 80 + 12$$
$$= 322$$

Modified Repeated Addition

Many children are taught to think of whole-number multiplication as repeated addition. However, using repeated addition as a computation method is inefficient for anything but small numbers. For example, it would be extremely tedious to add fifty-three 67s in order to compute 67 × 53. Using a modified repeated-addition algorithm, in which multiples of 10, 100, and so on, are grouped together, can simplify the process.

Lattice Method

Everyday Mathematics initially included the lattice method for its recreational value and historical interest (it has been used since A.D. 1100 and appeared in the first printed arithmetic book, published in 1478) and because it provided practice with multiplication facts and adding single-digit numbers.

This method has become a favorite of many children in *Everyday Mathematics.*

It is not easy to explain why the method works, but it is very efficient. The following example shows how the method is used to find 67 × 53.

Example: Modified Repeated Addition

Think of 53 × 67 as fifty 67s plus three 67s. Since ten 67s is 670, fifty 67s is five 670s.

So, 53 × 67 is five 670s plus three 67s.

```
        67
      × 53
  ┌─  670
  │   670
  │   670
  ┤   670
  └─  670
  ┌─   67
  ┤    67
  └─   67
     ─────
     3,551
```

Example: Lattice Method

Follow these steps to find 67 × 53.

• Draw a 2-by-2 lattice, and write one factor along the top of the lattice and the other along the right. (Use a larger lattice to multiply numbers with more digits.)

• Draw diagonals from the upper-right corner of each box, extending beyond the lattice.

• Multiply each digit in one factor by each digit in the other. Write each product in the cell where the corresponding row and column meet. Write the tens digit of the product above the diagonal and the ones digit below the diagonal. For example, since 6 × 5 = 30, write 30 in the upper-left box with the 3 above the diagonal and the 0 below.

• Starting with the lower-right diagonal, add the numbers inside the lattice along each diagonal. If the sum along a diagonal is greater than 9, carry the tens digit to the next diagonal.

The first diagonal contains only 1, so the sum is 1. The sum on the second diagonal is 5 + 2 + 8 = 15. Write only the 5, and carry the 1 to the next column. The sum along the third diagonal is then 1 + 3 + 0 + 1, or 5. The sum on the fourth diagonal is 3.

• Read the product from the upper left to the lower right. The product is 3,551.

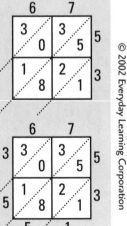

Division Algorithms

One type of division situation involves making as many equal-size groups as possible from a collection of objects: How many dozens can you make with 746 eggs? How many 5-passenger cars are needed for 37 people? Such problems ask, "How many of these are in that?" More generally, $a \div b$ can be interpreted as "How many bs are in a?" This idea forms the basis for the division algorithms presented in this section.

Partial-Quotients

The partial-quotients algorithm uses a series of "at least, but less than" estimates of how many bs are in a.

Example: Partial-Quotients
Estimate the number of 12s in 158.
You might begin with multiples of 10 because they are simple to work with. There are at least ten 12s in 158 ($10 \times 12 = 120$), but there are fewer than twenty ($20 \times 12 = 240$). Record 10 as a first guess, and subtract ten 12s from 158, leaving 38.

Now estimate the number of 12s in 38.
There are more than three ($3 \times 12 = 36$) but fewer than four ($4 \times 12 = 48$). Record 3 as the next guess, and subtract three 12s from 38, leaving 2.

Since 2 is less than 12, you can stop estimating. The final result is the sum of the guesses ($10 + 3 = 13$) plus what is left over (the remainder of 2).

```
    _____
12 )158      10    first guess
    120
     38       3    second guess
     36      ___
      2      13    sum of guesses
```

$$158 \div 12 \longrightarrow 13 \text{ R2}$$

Column Division

Column division is a simplification of the traditional long division algorithm you probably learned in school, but it is easier to learn. To use the method, you draw vertical lines separating the digits of the divisor and work one place-value column at a time.

Example: Column Division

To find 683 ÷ 5, imagine sharing $683 among 5 people. Think about having 6 hundred-dollar bills, 8 ten-dollar bills, and 3 one-dollar bills.

First, divide up the hundred-dollar bills. Each person gets one, and there is one left over.

$$
\begin{array}{r|r|r}
1 & & \\
\hline
5\overline{)6} & 8 & 3 \\
-\,5 & & \\
\hline
1 & &
\end{array}
$$

Trade the leftover hundred-dollar bill for 10 ten-dollar bills. Now you have a total of 18 ten-dollar bills. Each person gets 3, and there are 3 left over.

$$
\begin{array}{r|r|r}
1 & 3 & \\
\hline
5\overline{)6} & \cancel{8} & 3 \\
-\,5 & 18 & \\
\hline
\cancel{1} & -\,15 & \\
& 3 &
\end{array}
$$

Trade the 3 leftover ten-dollar bills for 30 one-dollar bills. You now have a total of 33 one-dollar bills. Each person gets 6, and there are 3 left over.

$$
\begin{array}{r|r|r}
1 & 3 & 6 \\
\hline
5\overline{)6} & \cancel{8} & \cancel{3} \\
-\,5 & 18 & 33 \\
\hline
\cancel{1} & -\,15 & -\,30 \\
& \cancel{3} & 3
\end{array}
$$

So, when you divide $683 among 5 people, each person gets $136, and there are $3 left over. So, 683 ÷ 5 = 136 R3.

What Is Assessment?

Because good assessment is essential to a child's education, you will find it to be an important part of the *Everyday Mathematics* program. Two of the most important purposes of assessment are:

- To reveal the development of the child's mathematical understanding.
- To provide useful feedback to the teacher about the child's instructional needs.

Effective educational programs contain strategies for collecting information about students' abilities and understand that teachers use this information on an ongoing basis. Good teachers use this information to make adjustments in their lessons, monitor the effectiveness of their classroom practice, adapt educational materials to the needs of their students, and report student progress.

What Is a "Balanced" Approach to Assessment?

All assessment plans should use a variety of techniques. *Everyday Mathematics* uses a balance of approaches that includes Ongoing, Product, and Periodic Assessment in varying proportions

depending on grade level, children's experience, time of year, and so on. The circle graph shown here is an example from third grade of the possible proportions of the use of these assessments.

Ongoing Assessment includes informal observations of children during teacher-guided instruction, strategy sharing, game play, and slate routines. The teacher may use brief mental notes, short written notes, or more elaborate record sheets to record these assessments.

Product Assessment may include samples of daily written work, group project reports, and mathematical writing and diagrams. Some of these products may be included in a child's portfolio.

Periodic Assessment includes more formal types of assessment, such as quizzes and end-of-unit written, oral, and slate assessments.

In addition, *Outside Tests* may be mandated by schools, districts, or states. These tests vary widely, from traditional standardized tests with multiple-choice responses to more performance-based assessments.

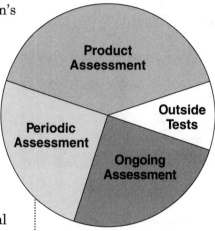

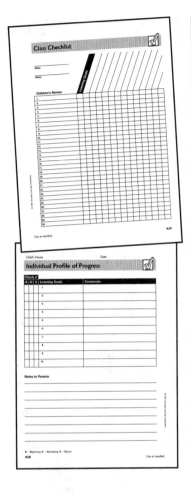

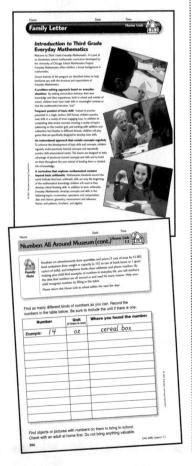

What Assessment Tools Are Built into *Everyday Mathematics*?

In order to achieve balanced, effective assessment, *Everyday Mathematics* provides a variety of tools and suggestions. The list below briefly describes a few.

- *Portfolios* can be used to store selections of a child's work. Usually, the teacher provides guidelines for what should be selected to provide a representative sample of work. Portfolios help children and teachers keep track of progress. Portfolios emphasize progress over time, rather than results at a given moment, and can involve children more directly in the assessment process.

- *Rubrics* are frameworks that help teachers gauge progress on various aspects of a child's learning. A simple but effective rubric that many teachers use is the classification of children as Beginning, Developing, or Secure with respect to a particular skill or concept.

- *Math Boxes* are pages in the *Student Math Journals* with practice problems. These pages are designed for independent work, but let children work with partners if appropriate. Math Boxes may be used to communicate with parents and guardians about the mathematics being taught and about individual children's strengths and weaknesses.

- *Exit Slips* are used by students to record responses to open-ended questions at the close of a lesson or unit.

- *Class Checklists* and *Individual Profiles of Progress* allow teachers to record children's progress in meeting specific learning goals.

- *Unit Reviews* and *Assessments* are provided at the end of each unit. Learning goals are listed along with suggestions for oral, slate, and written assessments.

- *Midyear and End-of-Year Assessments* provide additional opportunities that teachers may use as part of their balanced assessment plan.

How Can You Get Involved?

Communicate with your child's teacher on a regular basis. Attend school functions planned to inform you about *Everyday Mathematics* and your child's progress. If possible, volunteer to help with Explorations or Projects or to observe a lesson. At home, talk with your child about real-life situations that involve mathematics.

With each lesson, your child will usually bring home a corresponding Home Link (K-3) or Study Link (4-6). With each unit is a Family Letter. The activities in these Links are designed to build a strong bridge between home and school. Ask your child to "teach" you the mathematics lessons he or she is learning.

Study Links require older students to take initiative and responsibility for completing their assignments independently, although some Links may require the student to interact with someone outside the classroom.

Do-Anytime Activities for Grades K–3

Mathematics means more when it is rooted in real-life situations. The following activities allow children to practice mathematics skills while riding in a car, doing chores, helping with shopping, and performing other everyday routines. These "do-anytime" activities are organized by topic and grade level.

Visual Patterns, Number Patterns, and Counting

K Count the steps needed to walk from the sidewalk to the front door (or any two places). Try to walk the same distance with fewer steps or with more steps.

K Practice counting past the "100 number barrier." Start from different numbers, such as 81, 92, 68, and so on.

❶ Count orally by 2s, 5s, and 10s.

❶ Count and pair objects found around the house, and determine whether there's an odd or even number of items.

❷ Make a game out of doubling, tripling, and quadrupling small numbers.

❷ Ask your child to count by certain intervals. For example, "Start at zero, and count by 4s."

Addition, Subtraction, Multiplication, and Division

K Show your child three objects, and count them aloud together. Then put the objects in your pocket, a box, or a bag. Put two more objects in with the three objects, and ask your child, "How many are in there now?" Repeat with other numbers and with subtraction (taking objects out of the pocket, box, or bag).

K Make up "one more" and "one less" stories. Have your child use counters, such as pennies or raisins. For example, "The dinosaur laid 5 eggs." (Your child puts down 5 counters.) "Then the dinosaur laid one more egg." (Your child puts down another counter.) "How many eggs are there?"

❶ Using the number grid, select a number, and have your child point to the number that is 1 more or 1 less than the selected number. Do problems like this: "Count back (or up) 5 spaces. On which number do you land?"

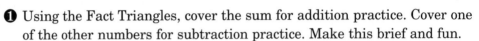
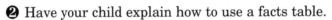

									0
1	2	3	4	5	6	7	8	9	10
11	12	13	14	15	16	17	18	19	20
21	22	23	24	25	26	27	28	29	30
31	32	33	34	35	36	37	38	39	40
41	42	43	44	45	46	47	48	49	50

❶ Using the Fact Triangles, cover the sum for addition practice. Cover one of the other numbers for subtraction practice. Make this brief and fun.

❷ Have your child explain how to use a facts table.

❸ Practice addition and subtraction fact extensions. For example,

$6 + 7 = 13$ $60 + 70 = 130$ $600 + 700 = 1,300$

❸ Provide your child with problems with missing factors for multiplication practice. For example, "6 times what number equals 18?"

Number Stories

K Encourage your child to figure out answers to real-life situations: "We have one can of tuna, and we need five. How many more do we need to buy?"

❶ Have your child tell you a number story that goes with a given number sentence, such as $4 + 2 = 6$.

❶ Ask for answers to number stories that involve two or more items. For example, "I want to buy a doughnut for 45 cents and a juice box for 89 cents. How much money do I need?" ($1.34)

❷ Make up number stories involving estimation. For example, pretend that your child has $2.00 and that he or she wants to buy a pencil marked 64¢, a tablet marked 98¢, and an eraser marked 29¢. Help your child to estimate the total cost of the three items (without tax) and to determine if there is enough money to buy them.

❷ Take turns making up multiplication and division number stories to solve. Share solution strategies.

❸ Ask questions that involve equal sharing. For example, "Seven children share 49 baseball cards. How many cards does each child get?"

❸ Ask questions that involve equal groups. For example, "Pencils are packaged in boxes of 8. There are 3 boxes. How many pencils are there?"

Place Value

K Have your child press the number 3 on a calculator. Have him or her press another 3 and read the number. Repeat for 333 and 3,333.

❶ Say a 2- or 3-digit number. Then have your child identify the actual value of the digit in each place. For example, in the number 952, the value of the 9 is 900; the value of the 5 is 50; and the value of the 2 is 2 ones, or two.

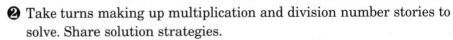

❷ Say a 3- or 4-digit number. Then have your child identify the actual value of the digit in each place. For example, in the number 3,587, the value of the 3 is 3,000; the value of the 5 is 500; the value of the 8 is 80; and the value of the 7 is 7 ones, or 7.

❸ Write decimals for your child to read, such as 0.32 (thirty-two hundredths) and 0.9 (nine-tenths).

Thousands	Hundreds	Tens	Ones		Tenths	Hundredths	Thousandths
1,000	100	10	1	.	.1	.01	.001

Money and Time

K Start a family penny jar, and collect your family's pennies. Count them from time to time.

K Teach your child how to set the kitchen timer when you are cooking.

❶ Count various sets of nickels and pennies together.

❶ Have your child tell you the time as "minutes after the hour."

❷ Gather a handful of coins with a value less than $2. Have your child calculate the total value.

❷ Ask the time throughout the day. Encourage alternate ways of naming time, such as *twenty to nine* for 8:40 and *half past two* for 2:30.

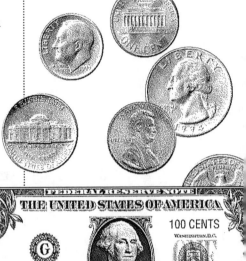

❸ Have your child write the following amounts using a dollar sign and decimal point: 4 dollar bills, 3 dimes, and 2 pennies; 4 dimes and 8 pennies; 3 dollar bills and 8 dimes; 8 pennies.

❸ Draw an analog clock face with the hour and minute hands showing 8 o'clock. Ask your child to write the time shown. Repeat with other times, such as 3:30, 11:45, 7:10, and so on.

Measurement

K Arrange various objects (books, boxes, and cans) by various size and measure (length, weight, and volume) attributes. Talk with your child about how they are arranged using comparison words like *taller, shorter, narrower, wider, heaviest, lightest, more, less, about,* and *the same.*

K Record family heights by marking them on a door frame. Record in centimeters as well as inches. Measure again in the same location several months later.

❶ Use a standard measuring tool (a ruler, a tape measure, or a yardstick) to measure objects located in the house. Keep an ongoing list of items measured and their approximate lengths and widths using inches.

❷ Discuss household tools that can be used to measure things or help solve mathematical problems.

❷ Gather a tape measure, a yardstick, a ruler, a cup, a gallon container, and a scale. Discuss the various things you and your child can measure with each. Compare to see which is the best tool for different types of measurement. For example, "What would you use to measure the length of a room: a tape measure, a yardstick, or a ruler?"

❸ Review equivalent names for measurements. For example, "How many cups in a pint?"

Fractions

K As you cut a pizza into equal pieces, count the pieces, and describe the pieces with their fraction names. For example, if you cut a pizza into four pieces, then each piece is $\frac{1}{4}$ of the whole pizza.

K Compare the sizes of the pieces as you divide a pizza into smaller and smaller sections. "Is $\frac{1}{2}$ of the pizza smaller or larger than $\frac{1}{4}$ of the pizza?"

❶ Count out eight pennies (or any type of counter, such as beans or macaroni). Ask your child to show you $\frac{1}{2}$ of the pennies and then $\frac{1}{4}$ of the pennies. Do this with a variety of numbers.

❶ Give your child several pieces of paper to fold into halves, fourths, or eighths. He or she can label each part with the appropriate fraction symbol ($\frac{1}{2}$, $\frac{1}{4}$, $\frac{1}{8}$).

❷ Read a recipe, and discuss the fractions in it. For example, ask, "How many $\frac{1}{4}$ cups of sugar would we need to get 1 cup of sugar?"

❷ Compare two fractions, and tell which is larger. For example, ask, "Which would give you more of a pizza: $\frac{1}{8}$ of it or $\frac{1}{4}$?"

❸ Help your child find fractions in the everyday world—in advertisements, on measuring tools, in recipes, and so on.

❸ Draw name-collection boxes for various numbers, and together with your child, write five to ten equivalent names in each box. Include name-collection boxes for fractions and decimals. For example, a $\frac{1}{2}$ name-collection box might include $\frac{2}{4}$, $\frac{10}{20}$, 0.5, 0.50, $\frac{500}{1,000}$, and so on.

Geometry

K Play "I Spy" with your child. Begin with easy clues, and work up to more difficult ones. For example, "I spy something that is round." "I spy something that is round and has two hands." "I spy something that has four legs and is a rectangle."

K Look around the house for different geometric shapes, such as triangles, squares, circles, and rectangles.

❶ Look for geometric shapes around the house, at the supermarket, as part of architectural features, and on street signs. Begin to call these shapes by their geometric names.

❷ Look for 2- and 3-dimensional shapes in your home and neighborhood. Explore and name the shapes, and brainstorm about their characteristics.

❷ Use household items (such as toothpicks and marshmallows; straws; and twist-ties, sticks, and paper) to construct shapes.

❸ Begin a Shapes Museum, a collection of common objects that represent a variety of 2- and 3- dimensional shapes. Label the shapes.

❸ Search for geometric figures with your child. Identify them by name if possible, and talk about their characteristics. For example, a stop sign is an octagon, which has 8 sides and 8 angles. A brick is a rectangular prism, in which all faces are rectangles.

Do-Anytime Activities for Grades 4–6

Mathematics means more when it is rooted in real-life situations. The following activities allow children to practice mathematics skills while riding in a car, doing chores, helping with shopping, and performing other everyday routines. These "do-anytime" activities are organized by topic and grade level.

Addition, Subtraction, Multiplication, and Division

❹ Continue working on multiplication and division facts by using Fact Triangles and fact families or by playing games in the *Student Reference Book.*

❹ Give your child multidigit numbers to add and subtract, such as $427 + 234$, $72 - 35$, and $815 - 377$.

❺ Practice extending multiplication facts. Write each set of problems so that your child may recognize a pattern.

Set A	$6 * 10$	$6 * 100$	$6 * 1,000$
Set B	$5 * 10$	$5 * 100$	$5 * 1,000$
Set C	$10 [7s]$	$100 [7s]$	$1,000 [7s]$

❺ When your child adds or subtracts multidigit numbers, talk about the strategy that works best. Try not to impose the strategy that works best for you! Here are some problems to try:

$467 + 343 =$ _____ _____ $= 761 + 79$

$894 - 444 =$ _____ $842 - 59 =$ _____

❻ Consider allowing your child to double or triple recipes for you whenever you are planning to do that. Watch your child to make sure he or she does the math for every ingredient. Or your child can halve a recipe if your cooking plans call for smaller amounts.

❻ Have your child calculate the tip of a restaurant bill through mental math and estimation. For example, if the bill is $25 and you intend to tip 15%, have your child go through the following mental algorithm: 10% of $25.00 is $2.50. Half of $2.50 (5%) is $1.25. $2.50 (10%) + $1.25 (5%) would be a tip of $3.75 (15%). The total amount to leave on the table would be $28.75.

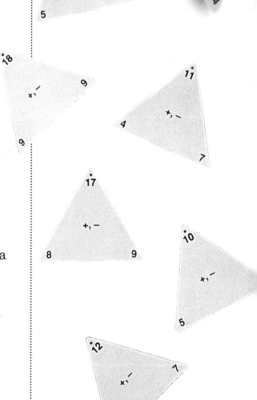

Fractions, Decimals, and Percents

❹ Have your child look for everyday uses of fractions and percents. Areas to explore would be games, grocery or fabric stores, cookbooks, measuring cups and spoons, the evening news, and statistics in newspapers.

❹ Encourage your child to incorporate such terms as *whole, halves, thirds,* and *fourths* into his or her everyday life.

❺ Write whole numbers and decimals for your child to read, such as 650 *(six hundred fifty)* and 42.5 *(forty-two and five-tenths).* Ask your child to identify digits in the various places—thousands place, hundreds place, tens place, ones place, tenths place, hundredths place, and thousandths place.

❺ Help your child identify advertisements in signs, newspapers, and magazines that use percents. Help your child find the sale price of an item that is discounted by a certain percent. For example, a $40 shirt that is reduced by 25% is $30.

❻ Encourage your child to incorporate the vocabulary of fractions and decimals into his or her everyday speech. Make sure he or she understands that one-tenth is equivalent to 10%; quarter, to 25%; three-quarters, to 75%; and so on.

❻ Encourage your child to read nutrition labels. Have him or her calculate the percent of fat in the item.

$$\frac{\text{fat calories}}{\text{total calories}} = \frac{\text{percent of fat (?)}}{100\%}$$

Your child should use cross-multiplication to solve the problem.

Measurement

❹ Work with your child on drawing a scale map of your city, town, or neighborhood, or have your child do a scale drawing of the floor plan of your house or apartment.

❺ Encourage your child to develop his or her own set of personal measures for both metric and U.S. customary units.

❺ Encourage your child to create his or her own mnemonics, or sayings, to help in remembering conversion measurements. Start with "A pint's a pound the world 'round," and have your child create his or her own from there.

❻ If you have carpentry hobbies, consider allowing your child to measure, cut, or add and subtract measures for you. Expect him or her to be able to measure to the nearest eighth of an inch and to be able to add and subtract such measures.

❻ If you are planning to paint or carpet a room, consider allowing your child to measure and calculate the area. Have him or her write the formula for Area (Area = length * width) and show you the calculations. If the room is an irregular shape, divide it into separate rectangular regions, and have your child find the area of each one. If a wall has a cathedral ceiling, imagine a line across the top of the wall to form a triangle. Your child can use the formula $\frac{1}{2}$ * base * height = A to calculate the area of the triangle.

© 2002 Everyday Learning Corporation

Geometry Explorations

❹ Help your child recognize and identify real-world examples of right angles (the corner of a book) and parallel lines (railroad tracks).

❹ Encourage your child to identify and classify acute (less than 90°), obtuse (between 90° and 180°), right (90°), straight (180°), and reflex (between 180° and 360°) angles in everyday things (the architecture of a building, a bridge, a ramp, or a house).

❹ Have your child compile a shapes portfolio or create a collage of labeled shapes. Images can be taken from newspapers, magazines, and photographs.

❺ When you are at home or at a store, ask your child to identify different types of polygons, such as triangles, squares, pentagons, and hexagons.

❺ Ask your child to identify 2-dimensional and 3-dimensional shapes around the house.

❻ Ask your child to find apparent right angles or other types of angles: acute (less than 90°) and obtuse (between 90° and 180°). Guide your child to look particularly at bridge supports for a variety of angles.

❻ While you are driving in the car together, direct your child to look for congruent figures (figures with the same size and shape): Windows in office buildings, circles on stop lights, many street signs, and so on, are all congruent figures.

Patterns and Algebra Concepts

❹ Have your child look for frieze patterns on buildings, rugs, floors, and clothing. Have your child make sketches of friezes that he or she sees.

❹ If your child has an interest in music, encourage him or her to study the mathematical qualities of the patterns of notes and rhythms. Composers of even the simplest tunes use reflections and translations of notes and chords (groups of notes).

❺ Review tessellations with your child. Encourage your child to name the regular tessellations and to draw and name the eight semiregular tessellations. Challenge your child to create nonpolygonal Escher-type translation tessellations. You may want to go to the library first and show your child examples of Escher's work.

Data, Chance, and Probability

❹ Help your child look up the population and land area of the state and city in which you live and compare these facts with those of other states and cities.

❹ Encourage your child to recognize the language of probability used in everyday situations, such as weather reports and scientific findings. Have your child make a list of things that could never happen, things that might happen, and things that are sure to happen.

❺ Visit the Web site for the U.S. Bureau of the Census at http://www.census.gov/. Have your child write three interesting pieces of information that he or she learned from the Web site.

❺ Have your child keep a running tally of when the school bus arrives. Or have your child time him- or herself to see how long it takes to walk to school in the morning compared to walking home in the afternoon. After a week, have your child plot the times, look for variations, and try to describe the times by using an equation.

❻ While playing a game that uses a die, keep a tally sheet of how many times a certain number lands. For example, find how many times during the game the number 5 comes up. Have your child write the probability for the chosen number. ($\frac{1}{6}$ is the probability that any given number on a six-sided die will land.) The tally sheet should show how many times the die was rolled during the game and how many times the chosen number came up.

❻ Watch with your child for events that occur without dependence on any other event. In human relationships, truly independent events may be difficult to isolate, but this observation alone helps to define the random events in games. Guide your child to see the difference between dependent events and random events. For example, "Will Uncle Mike come for dinner?" depends on whether or not he got his car fixed. However, "Will I get heads or tails when I flip this coin?" depends on no other event.

Frequently Asked Questions

Parent Involvement

Q: How can I get involved? How can I reinforce my child's mathematics learning at home?

A: Communicate with your child's teacher on a regular basis. If possible, volunteer to help with Explorations or Projects or to observe a lesson. Attend school functions, such as Math Night, planned to inform you about *Everyday Mathematics* and your child's progress. At home, talk with your child about real-life situations that involve mathematics, such as buying groceries or balancing the checkbook. Ask your child to "teach" you the mathematics lessons he is learning, including favorite games and creative solution strategies. Ask your child to bring home the Grade 3, 4, 5, or 6 *Student Reference Books* to share together.

Basic Facts

Q: Will my child learn and practice basic facts?

A: Your child will learn and practice all of the basic facts in many different ways without having to complete an overwhelming number of drill pages. She will play mathematics games in which numbers are generated randomly by dice, dominoes, spinners, or cards. She will work with Fact Triangles, which present fact families and stress the addition/subtraction and multiplication/division relationships. In fourth grade, she will take timed "50-facts" multiplication tests that will require her to learn the facts she does not already know. She will have continuing access to addition/subtraction and multiplication/division fact tables that will serve as references for the facts she does not yet know and as records of the facts she does. She will also take part in short oral drills to review facts with her classmates.

Computation

Q: Does my child have opportunities to learn, develop, and practice computation skills?

A: Your child gains the fact knowledge he needs for computation from basic facts practice. He solves problems in a meaningful way through number stories about real-life situations that require him to understand the need for computation, which operations to use, and how to use those operations. He often has the opportunity to develop and explain his own strategies for solving problems through algorithm invention. He practices mental arithmetic during Minute Math and 5-Minute Math. He also performs activities that encourage him to round or estimate numbers mentally.

Focus Algorithms

Q: What are focus algorithms?

A: Children spend a lot of time in the early stages of learning about computation experimenting with and sharing their own problem-solving methods instead of simply learning a set of prescribed standard algorithms. *Everyday Mathematics* also includes a focus algorithm for each operation—addition, subtraction, multiplication, and division. These algorithms are powerful and relatively efficient, and most are easier to understand and learn than traditional algorithms. All children are expected to master the focus algorithm for each operation. Once they show they have mastered it, they are free to use any method to solve problems. Given a choice, however, most children prefer their own procedures.

Mastery

Q: Why does my child have to move on to the next lesson if he hasn't mastered skills in the current lesson?

A: Mastery varies with each child and depends on his learning style and problem-solving style. Because people rarely master a new concept or skill after only one exposure, the program has a repeated-exposure approach that informally introduces topics for two years before formal study. This approach offers both consistent follow-up and a variety of experiences. If your child does not master a topic the first time it is introduced, he will have the opportunity to increase his understanding the next time it is presented. Your child will regularly review and practice new concepts by playing content-specific games and by completing written exercises and assessments.

Addressing Individual Needs

Q: My child has special needs. Will she be able to succeed in the program? How can the program address her individual needs?

A: *Everyday Mathematics* is designed to be flexible and to offer many opportunities for teachers to meet the varying needs of each child. There are many open-ended activities that will allow your child to succeed at her current skill level. While playing games, inventing algorithms, writing number stories, and solving problems in Minute Math and Math Boxes exercises, your child will develop her strengths and improve in the weak areas. Furthermore, your child's teacher may group students to best suit their needs. The teacher may also modify or adjust program material according to student needs.

Games

Q: Why does my child play games in class?

A: *Everyday Mathematics* games reinforce concepts in a valuable and enjoyable way. They are designed to help your child practice his basic facts and computation skills and develop increasingly sophisticated solution strategies. These games also lay the foundation for learning increasingly difficult concepts. Certain games give your child experience using a calculator, while other games emphasize the relationship between the money system and place value. Your child may play *Everyday Mathematics* games at home from time to time. Spend some time learning the games, and you will understand how much they contribute to your child's mathematics progress.

Assessment

Q: How do you measure my child's progress? What can you show me that demonstrates what she has learned?

A: *Everyday Mathematics* teachers assess understanding periodically and on an ongoing basis. Teachers frequently make detailed written observations of students' progress as they watch students working on Math Boxes or slate activities. They also evaluate students' responses to Minute Math, interactions during group work or games, and written responses to Math Messages. Teachers use unit review and assessment pages to evaluate individual student progress. Instead of sending home traditional grade reports, the teacher may show you a rubric—a framework for tracking your child's progress. The rubric may be divided into categories describing different skill levels, such as Beginning, Developing, and Secure. Using these categories, the teacher indicates your child's skill in and understanding of a particular mathematical topic. The teacher can use this record of progress to decide which areas need review and whether certain students need additional help or challenge.

Calculators

Q: Why is my child using a calculator? Will he become dependent on the calculator for solving problems?

A: Your child uses a calculator to learn concepts, recognize patterns, develop estimation skills, and explore problem solving. He learns when a calculator can help solve problems beyond his current paper-and-pencil capabilities. He learns that in some situations, he can rely on his own problem-solving power to get an answer more quickly. Your child also uses basic fact and operations knowledge and estimation skills to determine whether the calculator's solution is reasonable. He becomes comfortable with the calculator as one technological tool.

Standardized Tests

Q: How do you help your class prepare for standardized tests?

A: *Everyday Mathematics* teachers help students prepare for standardized tests by giving timed tests more frequently and by spending more time on the *Everyday Mathematics* games that reinforce basic facts. Teachers also review test-taking strategies, such as looking for reasonableness in an answer.

Literature List for Grades K–3

These mathematics-related literature titles are organized by mathematical topics. Some titles may appear more than once.

*These titles are out of print. Check your local library.

Visual Patterns, Number Patterns, and Counting

*Amazing Anthony Ant**
Lorna and Graham Philpot
Random House, 1994

Anno's Counting Book
Mitsumasa Anno
Harper & Row, 1999

*Anno's Counting House**
Mitsumasa Anno
Philomel, 1982

Can You Count Ten Toes? Count to 10 in 10 Different Languages
Lezlie Evans
Houghton Mifflin Company, 1999

City by Numbers
Stephen T. Johnson
Penguin Putnam Books for Young Readers, 1998

Count Your Way through Japan
Jim Haskins
Carlrhoda Books, Inc., 1987

Count Your Way through Korea
Jim Haskins
Carlrhoda Books, Inc., 1989

Counting on Calico
Phyllis Tildes
Charlesbridge Publishing, 1995

The Crayon Counting Book
Pam Munoz Ryan
Charlesbridge Publishing, 1996

Ed Emberley's Picture Pie: A Circle Drawing Book
Ed Emberley
Little, Brown, 1984

Fish Eyes: A Book You Can Count On
Lois Ehlert
Harcourt Brace, 1990

How Many Bugs in a Box?
David A. Carter
Scholastic, 1994

How Much Is a Million?
David M. Schwartz
Lothrop, Lee & Shepard Books, 1993

I Spy Two Eyes: Numbers in Art
Lucy Micklethwait
Greenwillow Books, 1998

Moira's Birthday
Robert Munsch
Annick Press, 1987

Moja Means One
Muriel Feelings
Dial Books, 1971

Visual Patterns, Number Patterns, and Counting (continued)

Mouse Count
Ellen Stoll Walsh
Voyager Books, 1995

My First Number Book
Marie Heinst
Dorling Kindersley, 1992

Numbers at Play: A Counting Book*
Charles Sullivan
Rizzoli International Publications, 1992

1, 2, 3
Tana Hoban
Morrow, William & Co., 1985

Out for the Count*
Kathryn Cave
Simon and Schuster, 1991

The Right Number of Elephants
Jeff Sheppard
Scholastic, 1990

17 Kings and 42 Elephants
Margaret Mahy
Dial Books, 1993

Ten Apples Up on Top
Theo LeSieg (Dr. Suess)
Random House, 1987

Ten Black Dots
Donald Crews
Scholastic, 1995

Ten, Nine, Eight
Molly Bang
Mulberry Books, 1991

The 329th Friend*
Marjorie W. Sharmat
Four Winds Press, 1992

12 Ways to Get to 11
Eve Merriam
Simon and Schuster, 1996

Two Ways to Count to Ten: A Liberian Folktale
Ruby Dee
Henry Holt and Co., 1990

Addition, Subtraction, Multiplication, and Division

Anno's Mysterious Multiplying Jar
Masaichiro Anno
Philomel Books, 1999

Bunches and Bunches of Bunnies
Louise Mathews
Scholastic, 1999

Cactus Desert, Arctic Tundra, and *Tropical Rain Forest* (from the One Small Square series)
Donald Silver
McGraw, 1997

The King's Chessboard
David Birch
Penguin Putnam Books for Young Readers, 1993

The M & M's® Counting Book
Barbara Barbieri McGrath
Charlesbridge Publishing, 1994

Number One Number Fun
Kay Chorao
Holiday House, 1995

One Hundred Hungry Ants
Elinor J. Pinczes
Houghton Mifflin Company, 1995

Sea Squares
Joy N. Hulme
Hyperion Paperbacks, 1993

Welcome to the Green House
Jane Yolen
Putnam Publishing Group, 1997

Welcome to the Ice House
Jane Yolen
Putnam Publishing Group, 1997

Number Stories

The Doorbell Rang
Pat Hutchins
Greenwillow Books, 1986

Mission: Addition
Loreen Leedy
Holiday House, 1997

Place Value

Anno's Counting Book
Mitsumasa Anno
Harper & Row, 1999

The Cheerios® Counting Book
Barbara Barbieri McGrath
Scholastic, 1998

A Fair Bear Share
Stuart J. Murphy
HarperCollins Publishers, 1998

Mission: Addition
Loreen Leedy
Holiday House, 1997

Money and Time

Alexander, Who Used to Be Rich Last Sunday
Judith Viorst
Atheneum, 1978

Benny's Pennies
Pat Brisson
Atheneum, 1995

A Chair for My Mother
Vera Williams
Econo-Clad Books, 1999

Chicken Soup with Rice
Maurice Sendack
Scholastic, 1991

Clocks and More Clocks
Pat Hutchins
Aladdin Books, 1994

The Go-Around Dollar
Barbara Johnston Adams
Four Winds Press, 1992

How the Second Grade Got $8,205.50 to Visit the Statue of Liberty
Nathan Zimelman
Albert Whitman and Co., 1992

If You Made a Million
David M. Schwartz
Lothrop, Lee & Shepard Books, 1989

My First Book of Time
Claire Llewellyn
Dorling Kindersley, 1996

*Picking Peas for a Penny**
Angela Shelf Medearis
Scholastic, 1990

Pigs on a Blanket
Amy Axelrod
Simon and Schuster, 1998

Three Days on a River in a Red Canoe
Vera B. Williams
Scholastic, 1984

You Are Cordially Invited to P. Bear's New Year's Party! (Formal Dress Required): A Counting Book
Paul Owen Lewis
Beyond Words Publishing, 1989

Measurement

The Baker's Dozen: A Saint Nicholas Tale
Aaron Shepard
Atheneum, 1995

*A Flower Grows**
Ken Robbins
Dial Books, 1990

How Big Is a Foot?
Rolf Myller
Bantam Doubleday, 1999

Inch by Inch
Leo Lionni
Scholastic, 1995

*Mr. Archimedes' Bath**
Pamela Allen
HarperCollins Publishers, 1991

Pancakes, Pancakes!
Eric Carle
Scholastic, 1998

Papa, Please Get the Moon for Me
Eric Carle
Scholastic, 1986

*Picking Peas for a Penny**
Angela Shelf Medearis
Scholastic, 1990

*Super, Super, Superwords**
Bruce McMillan
Lothrop, Lee & Shepard, 1989

Fractions

Eating Fractions
Bruce McMillan
Scholastic, 1991

Fraction Action
Loreen Leedy
Holiday House, 1996

Fraction Fun
David A. Adler
Holiday House, 1996

Gator Pie
Louise Mathews
Sundance, 1995

Geometry

City by Numbers
Stephen T. Johnson
Penguin Putnam Books for Young Readers, 1998

A Cloak for a Dreamer
Aileen Friedman
Scholastic, 1995

Color Zoo
Lois Ehlert
HarperCollins Publishers, 1997

Fraction Action
Loreen Leedy
Holiday House, 1996

Grandfather Tang's Story
Ann Tompert
Crown Publishers, 1997

The Greedy Triangle
Marilyn Burns
Scholastic, 1995

*Linus the Magician**
Rosalie Barker
Harbor House of Publishers, 1993

Sea Shapes
Suse MacDonald
Gulliver Books, 1994

The Secret Birthday Message
Eric Carle
Harper Trophy, 1991

The Shape of Things
Dayle Ann Dodds
Candlewick Press, 1996

Shape Space
Cathryn Falwell
Clarion Books, 1992

Shapes, Shapes, Shapes
Tana Hoban
Greenwillow Books, 1986

Geometry (continued)

Space Race
Bob Barner
Bantam Doubleday, 1995

What Am I? Looking through Shapes at Apples and Grapes
N. N. Charles
The Blue Sky Press, 1994

Algebra and Uses of Variables

Corduroy
Don Freeman
Viking Press, 1976

*Eye Spy: A Mysterious Alphabet**
Linda Bourke
Chronicle Books, 1991

*Numblers**
Suse MacDonald
Dial Books, 1998

Puzzlers
Bill Oakes
Dial Books, 1989

Data and Chance

Caps for Sale
Esphyr Slobodkina
HarperCollins Publishers, 1996

Cloudy with a Chance of Meatballs
Judi Barrett
Atheneum, 1982

Harriet's Halloween Candy
Nancy Carlson
Puffin Books, 1997

Moira's Birthday
Robert Munsch
Annick Press, 1987

Purple, Green and Yellow
Robert Munsch
Annick Press, 1992

Patterns and Sequences

*The Amazing Book of Shapes**
Lydia Sharman
Dorling Kindersley, 1994

The Boy and the Quilt
Shirley Kurtz
Good Books, 1991

Eight Hands Round: A Patchwork Alphabet
Ann Whitford Paul
HarperCollins Publishers, 1999

The Patchwork Quilt
Valerie Flournoy
Scholastic, 1985

Sam Johnson and the Blue Ribbon Quilt
Lisa Campbell Ernst
Lothrop, Lee & Shepard Books, 1992

Ten Little Rabbits
Virginia Grossman
Chronicle Books, 1995

Literature List for Grades 4–6

These mathematics-related literature titles are organized by mathematical topics. Some titles may appear more than once.

*These titles are out of print. Check your local library.

Addition, Subtraction, Multiplication, and Division

Anno's Mysterious Multiplying Jar
Masaichiro Anno
Philomel Books, 1999

Arithmetic
Carl Sandburg
Harcourt Brace, 1993

The King's Chessboard
David Birch
Penguin Putnam Books for Young Readers, 1993

Math Curse
Jon Scieszka
Viking Children's Books, 1995

One Grain of Rice: A Mathematical Folktale
Demi
Scholastic, 1997

2 × 2 = Boo!
Loreen Leedy
Holiday House, 1996

Fractions, Decimals, and Percents

Fraction Action
Loreen Leedy
Holiday House, 1996

Gator Pie
Louise Mathews
Sundance, 1995

Measurement

A Chair for My Mother
Vera Williams
Econo-Clad Books, 1999

If You Made a Million
David M. Schwartz
Lothrop, Lee & Shepard, 1989

Incredible Comparisons
Russell Ash
Dorling Kindersley, 1996

Is a Blue Whale the Biggest Thing There Is?
Robert E. Wells
Albert Whitman, 1993

Measurement (continued)

The Librarian Who Measured the Earth
Kathryn Lasky
Little Brown and Company, 1994

The Magic School Bus Inside the Earth
Joanna Cole
Viking, 1995

Math Curse
Jon Scieszka
Viking Children's Books, 1995

Mr. Archimedes' Bath
Pamela Allen
HarperCollins Publishers, 1991

Spaghetti and Meatballs for All!
A Mathematical Story
Marilyn Burns
Scholastic, 1997

What's Smaller Than a Pygmy Shrew?
Robert E. Wells
Albert Whitman, 1995

Geometry Explorations

The Boy Who Reversed Himself
William Sleator
Puffin Books, 1998

Flatland: The Classic Speculation on Life in Four Dimensions
Edwin Abbott
HarperCollins Publishers, 1994

The Fly on the Ceiling: A Math Myth
Dr. Julie Glass
Econo-Clad Books, 1999

Grandfather Tang's Story
Ann Tompert
Crown Publishers, 1997

Julia Morgan, Architect of Dreams
Ginger Wadsworth
Lerner, 1990

Round Trip
Ann Jonas
Greenwillow Books, 1999

*Shape: The Purpose of Forms**
Eric Laithwaite
Franklin Watts, 1986

Sir Cumference and the First Round Table
Cindy Neuschwander and Wayne Geehan
Charlesbridge Publishing, 1997

Patterns and Algebra Concepts

Eight Hands Round: A Patchwork Alphabet
Ann Whitford Paul
HarperCollins Publishers, 1999

Esio Trot
Roald Dahl
Viking, 1999

A Grain of Rice
Helena Clare Pittman
Bantam Doubleday, 1996

The Mirror Puzzle Book
Marion Walter
Parkwest, 1985

Patterns in the Wild
National Wildlife Federation
National Wildlife Federation

The Quilt-Block History of Pioneer Days
Mary Cobb
The Millbrook Press, 1995

The Seasons Sewn: A Year in Patchwork
Ann Whitford Paul
Harcourt Brace, 2000

Teaching Tessellating Art
Jill Britton
Dale Seymour Publications, 1991

Visual Magic
David Thomson
Dial Books, 2000

Data, Chance, and Probability

Calculation and Chance
Laura Buller
Marshal Cavendish Corp., 1994

Do You Wanna Bet? Your Chance to Find Out about Probability
Jean Cushman
Clarion Books, 1991

How to Get Fabulously Rich
Thomas Rockwell
Franklin Watts, 1990

Incredible Comparisons
Russell Ash
Dorling Kindersley, 1996

*Socrates and the Three Little Pigs**
Mitsumasa Anno and Tsuyoshi Mori
Philomel Books, 1986

*What Do You Mean by "Average"? Means, Medians, & Modes**
Elizabeth James
Lothrop, Lee & Shepard Books, 1978

Numeration and Order

The Adventures of Penrose the Mathematical Cat
Theoni Pappas
World Wide Publishing (Tetra), 1997

Counting on Frank
Rod Clement
Gareth Stevens, 1991

*Every Number Is Special**
Henry Boyd
Dale Seymour Publications, 1985

G Is for Googol: A Math Alphabet Book
David M. Schwartz
Tricycle Press, 1998

How Much Is a Million?
David M. Schwartz
Lothrop, Lee & Shepard Books, 1993

Math Curse
Jon Scieszka
Viking Children's Books, 1995

Math Talk: Mathematical Ideas in Poems for Two Voices
Theoni Pappas
Wide World Publishing (Tetra), 1991

The Token Gift
Hugh William McKibbon
Annick, 1996

Zillions Magazine
No longer published, but its Web site is maintained:
http://www.zillions.org

Reference Frames

Around the World in Eighty Days
Jules Verne
William Morrow, 1996

The Magic School Bus Inside the Human Body
Joanna Cole
Scholastic, 1990

Rain Forest
Barbara Taylor
Dorling Kindersley, 1992

*Somewhere Today**
Bert Kitchen
Candlewick Press, 1994

Stephen Biesty's Incredible Cross-Sections
Stephen Biesty, Richard Platt
Random House, 1992

Stephen Biesty's Incredible Explosions
Stephen Biesty, Richard Platt
Random House, 1992

Home Connection Handbook
Glossary for Grades K–3

"about 3 times" circle rule The circumference of a circle is a little more than 3 times the length of its diameter.

addend One of two or more numbers that are added.

addition facts Two 1-digit numbers and their sum, such as $8 + 2 = 10$.

algorithm A step-by-step set of instructions for doing something, such as carrying out a computation or solving a problem.

A.M. An abbreviation that comes from *ante meridiem*, which means "before the middle of the day." It refers to the period between midnight and noon.

analog clock A clock that shows the time by the position of the hour and minute hands.

angle A figure that is formed by two rays or two line segments that have the same endpoint.

apex In a pyramid or cone, the vertex opposite the base.

area The measure of a bounded surface. Area is measured in square units.

array A rectangular arrangement of objects in rows and columns.

arrow-path puzzles Pieces of the number grid used to reinforce the structure of our base-ten numeration system.

bar graph A graph that shows the relationships among data by the use of bars to represent quantities.

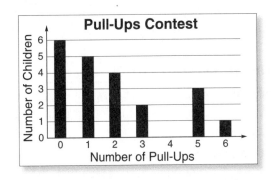

base A name used for the side of a polygon.

capacity A measure of pourable substances that take the shape of their containers, such as liquids, sand, and rice.

Celsius The temperature scale used in the metric system.

change diagram A device used to organize information in a change-to-more or change-to-less number story.

Start	Change	End
14	−5	?

change-to-more number story A number story having a starting quantity that is increased so that the ending quantity is more than the starting quantity.

circumference The distance around a circle.

comparison diagram A convenient way to represent a comparison number story.

Quantity
12

Quantity	Difference
9	?

comparison number story A number story that involves the difference between two quantities. For example: Ross sold 12 cookies. Anthony sold 5 cookies. How many more cookies did Ross sell?

cone A 3-dimensional shape with a curved surface, a circular face (base), and one vertex (corner).

coordinate grid A device for locating points in a plane. It is formed by drawing two number lines at right angles to each other that intersect at their zero points.

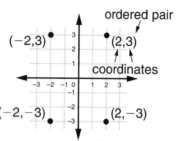

coordinates Ordered pairs of numbers written within parentheses and used to locate points on a coordinate grid.

counting numbers The numbers used in counting: {1, 2, 3, 4, ...}. Sometimes zero is included.

cube A polyhedron with six square faces.

cubic centimeter (cm³) A unit for measuring volume.

cylinder A 3-dimensional shape with a curved surface and two parallel circular or elliptical faces (bases) that are the same size.

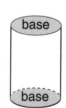

data A collection of information gathered by observing, counting, or measuring.

decimal point The mark that separates the whole from the fraction in decimal notation. In money amounts, it separates the dollar from the fractions of a dollar (the cents).

degree A unit of measure for angles. Also, a unit of measure for temperature.

denominator The total number of equal parts into which the unit or whole is divided.

diameter A line segment that passes through the center of a circle or sphere and has endpoints on the circle or sphere.

digits The symbols from 0 through 9 that are used to record any number in our numbering system.

dividend The amount before sharing in division.

divisor The number that divides another number. In 35 ÷ 7 = 5, the divisor is 7.

doubles fact The sum or product of the same two 1-digit numbers. For example, 5 + 5 = 10 or 3 × 3 = 9.

edge A line segment or curve where the surfaces of a solid meet.

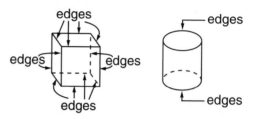

endpoint The point at the end of a ray or line segment.

equal groups Sets with the same number of elements.

equilateral triangle A triangle with all three sides the same length and all three angles the same measure.

equivalent fractions Different fractions that represent the same quantity. For example, $\frac{1}{2}$ and $\frac{3}{6}$ are equivalent fractions.

equivalent names Different ways of naming the same number. For example, 2 + 6, 4 + 4, 12 − 4, 100 − 92, 5 + 1 + 2, eight, VIII, and ⌿⌿⌿ /// are equivalent names for 8.

even number A whole number that ends in 0, 2, 4, 6, or 8. An even number of objects can always be broken into pairs.

Exploration A small-group hands-on activity designed to introduce or extend a topic.

face A flat surface on a 3-dimensional shape.

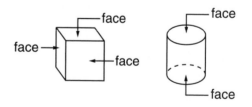

fact family A group of addition facts together with the subtraction facts. For example, 3 + 4 = 7, 4 + 3 = 7, 7 − 3 = 4, and 7 − 4 = 3 are a fact family.

fact power A term that refers to the ability to automatically recall basic number facts.

fact table A chart with rows and columns that shows all of the basic addition and subtraction facts or all of the basic multiplication and division facts.

Fact Triangles Cards with a triangle shape that show fact families; used like flash cards.

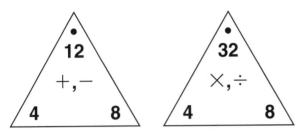

factor One of the numbers being multiplied in a multiplication number model.

Fahrenheit The temperature scale used in the U.S. customary system.

flat In *Everyday Mathematics,* the term for a base-10 block that represents 100 cm cubes.

fraction A number that names equal parts of a whole, or ONE.

fractional parts Equal parts of any whole.

Frames and Arrows Diagrams that are used to represent number sequences or sets of numbers that are ordered according to a rule. Each frame contains one of the numbers in the sequence. Each arrow stands for the rule that tells which number goes in the next frame.

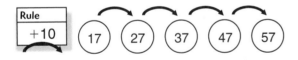

frequency The number of times an event or a value occurs in a set of data.

frequency table A chart on which data are tallied to find the frequency of given events or values.

Waist-to-floor measurement (inches)	Frequency	
	Tallies	Number
27	//	2
28		0
29	⊬⊬⊤	5
30	⊬⊬⊤ ///	8
31	⊬⊬⊤ //	7
32	////	4
	Total = 26	

function machine A diagram of an imaginary machine programmed to process numbers according to a certain rule. A number (input) is put into the machine and is transformed into a second number (output) through the application of a rule.

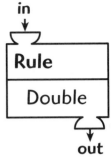

geometric solid A 3-dimensional shape bounded by surfaces. Common geometric solids include cones, spheres, and cylinders.

intersect To meet or cross.

kite A 4-sided polygon with two pairs of equal sides. The equal sides are next to each other. The four sides cannot all have the same length, so a rhombus is not a kite.

label A unit, descriptive word, or phrase used to put a number or numbers in context. Using a label reinforces the idea that numbers always refer to something.

lattice method One method for solving multidigit multiplication problems.

length The measure of the distance between two points.

line A straight path that goes on forever in both directions.

linear measure A measure used to designate length.

line graph A drawing that shows the relationships among data by using a set of points connected by line segments; often used to show trends.

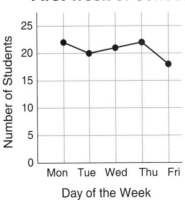

line plot A sketch of data that uses Xs, checks, or other marks above a number line to show how many times each value appeared in the set of data.

line segment Part of a straight line connecting two points.

line symmetry The exact mirror image matching of two halves of a shape.

long A base-10 block that represents ten.

Math Boxes A format for providing review problems and practicing skills.

Math Journal A book used by each child; it contains examples, instructions, and problems, as well as space, to record answers and observations.

Math Message An activity children complete independently, usually as a lead-in to the day's lesson.

mean An average number in a set of data. The mean is found by adding all of the data values and then dividing by the number of numbers in the set of data.

median The number in the middle when a set of data is organized in sequential order. If there is an even number of data points, the median is the mean of the two-middle values.

Mental Math and Reflexes A daily whole-class oral or written activity, often emphasizing computation done mentally.

metric system the system of measurement that uses millimeters, centimeters, meters, and kilometers for measuring length.

middle value Same as *median*.

millimeter In the metric system, a unit of length equivalent to $\frac{1}{10}$ of a centimeter and $\frac{1}{1,000}$ of a meter.

mixed number A name for a quantity consisting of a whole number and a fraction, such as $4\frac{1}{4}$.

mode The value that occurs most often in a set of data.

multiples Repeated groups of the same amount. Multiples of a number are the products of that number and whole numbers.

multiplication The operation used to find the total number of objects in several equal groups.

multiplication/division diagram A diagram used to represent numbers in which several groups are being considered together. The diagram has three parts: a number of groups, a number in each group, and a total number.

piles	cards per pile	cards in all
4	?	24

name-collection box A boxlike diagram tagged with a given number and used for collecting equivalent names for that number.

25	37 − 12	20 + 5

HHT HHT HHT HHT HHT

twenty-five   X X X X X

veinticinco   X X X X X

X X X X X

X X X X X

X X X X X

near doubles A strategy derived from the "doubles" facts. For example, a child might solve $3 + 4$ by noting that $3 + 3 = 6$, so $3 + 4$ must be 1 more than 6.

negative number A number less than 0; a number to the left of 0 on a horizontal number line.

number family A collection of addition and subtraction sentences, or multiplication and division sentences, made from the same three multidigit numbers.

number grid A table in which consecutive numbers are usually arranged in rows of ten.

number grid puzzle A piece of the number grid in which some but not all of the numbers are missing.

number model A numerical representation that shows how the parts of a number story are related. For example, $10 - 6 = 4$ is a number model for the following story: I had 10 brownies. I gave 6 away. How many did I have left?

number story A story made up by children, teachers, or parents. It contains a problem that can be solved by using one or more of the four basic operations.

Numbers All Around Museum A routine that promotes number awareness; used as the class assembles specific collections of numbers.

numerator The number above the fraction bar that indicates how many equal parts of the unit or whole are being considered.

odd number Any whole number that ends in 1, 3, 5, 7, or 9. When an odd number of objects is broken into pairs, there will always be one object that cannot be paired.

ordered number pair A pair of numbers used to locate points on a coordinate grid.

ordinal number A number used to express position or order in a series, such as first, third, or tenth.

parallel Always the same distance apart; never meeting.

parallelogram A 4-sided polygon with two pairs of parallel sides that are also the same length.

partial-products method One method for solving multiplication problems.

partial-sums method One method for solving addition problems.

parts-and-total diagram A device used to represent problems in which two or more quantities are combined to form a total quantity.

Total	
?	
Part	**Part**
8	5

parts-and-total number story A number story in which two parts are combined to find a total. A *parts-and-total diagram* can be used to keep track of the numbers and missing information in such problems.

Pattern-Block Template In *Everyday Mathematics*, a sheet of plastic with geometric shapes cut out, used to draw patterns and designs.

percent, % Per hundred; times $\frac{1}{100}$; times 0.01; 1 one-hundredth. For example, 15% means $\frac{15}{100}$ or 0.15 or 15 one-hundredths.

perimeter The distance around a bounded surface.

personal references Objects or distances that measure about 1 unit.

pie graph A graph in which a circle is divided into parts to represent the parts of a set of data. The circle represents the whole set of data.

place value The quantity a digit represents in a number. This quantity, or value, is determined by the digit's position in the number. For example, in the number 52, the 5 represents 5 tens, and the 2 represents 2 ones.

P.M. An abbreviation that comes from *post meridiem*. It refers to the period between noon and midnight.

point An exact location in space.

polygon A 2-dimensional figure with straight sides (line segments) connected end to end and no side crosses another side.

polyhedron A 3-dimensional geometric shape bounded by flat surfaces.

positive number A number greater than 0; a number to the right of 0 on a horizontal number line.

prime number A whole number greater than one that has exactly two whole-number factors: itself and 1. For example, 5 is a prime number because its only two factors are 5 and 1.

prism A 3-dimensional shape with two parallel flat faces (bases) that are the same size and shape.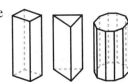

probability A number from 0 to 1 that is used to tell the chance of something happening.

product The result of doing multiplication.

pyramid A 3-dimensional shape in which one face (the base) is a polygon and the other faces are triangles with a common vertex (corner).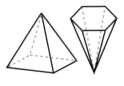

quadrangle A polygon that has four sides and four angles. Same as *quadrilateral*.

quadrilateral A polygon that has four sides and four angles. Same as *quadrangle*.

quotient The result when one number is divided by another number.

radius A line segment that goes from the center of a circle (or sphere) to any point on the circle.

random draw Each item being drawn has the same chance of being selected. For example, children will draw blocks from a bag and realize that each block has an equal chance of being selected.

range The difference between the greatest and least numbers in a set of data.

rational counting Counting using one-to-one matching, such as counting a number of objects.

ray A straight path that has one endpoint and goes on forever.

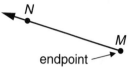

rectangle A parallelogram whose corners are all right angles.

remainder The amount left over when a number of things are divided into equal parts.

rhombus A parallelogram with all four sides the same length.

sphere A 3-dimensional shape with a curved surface that is, at all points, the same distance from its center point.

square centimeter (cm²) A unit for measuring area.

square number The product of a number multiplied by itself.

standard square unit A unit used to measure area.

standard unit A uniform unit of measure, such as inch and foot.

subtizing To perceive at a glance the number of items presented.

tally count Marks used to keep track of an amount counted or other data collected over a period of time.

Number of Pull-Ups	Number of Children
0	̶H̶H̶ /
1	̶H̶H̶
2	////
3	//
4	
5	///
6	/

temperature scales Columns of numbers found on thermometers. Most thermometers have both Fahrenheit and Celsius scales.

3-dimensional An object that does not lie completely within a single flat surface; an object with thickness as well as length and width.

tiling The covering of a surface with shapes so that there are no gaps or overlaps.

timeline A device for showing in sequence when events took place.

trade-first method (algorithm) A procedure for subtracting multidigit numbers.

turn-around facts Two addition (or multiplication) facts in which the order of the addends (or factors) is reversed. For example, 5 + 4 = 9 and 4 + 5 = 9.

2-dimensional A shape that lies completely within a plane, or flat surface.

unit boxes Boxes that contain labels or units of measure used in problems.

U.S. customary system The system of measurement that uses inches, feet, yards, and miles for measuring.

vertex The point at which the sides of a polygon or the edges of a polyhedron meet.

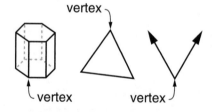

volume A measure of the amount of space taken up by a 3-dimensional object.

weight A measure of the force of gravity on an object or how heavy something is.

"What's My Rule?" A routine that consists of a set of number pairs in which the numbers in each pair are related to each other according to the same rule. The problems are usually displayed in table format in which two of the three parts are known. The goal is to find the unknown part.

Home Connection Handbook
Glossary for Grades 4–6

absolute value The distance between a number and 0 on the number line. The absolute value of a positive number is the number itself. The absolute value of a negative number is the *opposite* of the number. For example, the absolute value of 3 is 3, and the absolute value of –6 is 6. The absolute value of 0 is 0. The notation for the absolute value of a number *n* is $|n|$.

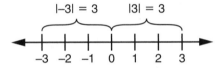

account balance An amount of money that you have or that you owe.

addend One of two or more numbers that are added. For example, in $5 + 3 + 1$, the addends are 5, 3, and 1.

adjacent angles Angles that are next to each other; adjacent angles have a common side but no other overlap. In the diagram, Angles 1 and 2 are adjacent angles. So are Angles 2 and 3, Angles 3 and 4, and Angles 4 and 1.

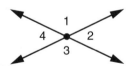

algebraic expression An expression that contains a variable. For example, if Maria is 2 inches taller than Joe and if the variable *M* represents Maria's height, then the algebraic expression $M - 2$ represents Joe's height. See also *expression*.

algorithm A set of step-by-step instructions for doing something, such as carrying out a computation or solving a problem.

angle A figure that is formed by two rays or two line segments with a common endpoint. The common endpoint is called the *vertex* of the angle. An *acute angle* has a measure greater than 0° and less than 90°. An *obtuse angle* has a measure greater than 90° and less than 180°. A *right angle* measures 90°. A *straight angle* measures 180°. See also *endpoint, ray,* and *vertex*. A *reflex angle* has a measure greater than 180° and less than 360°.

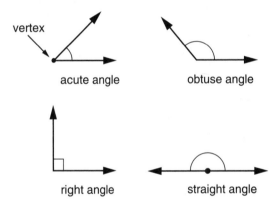

angle of separation A measure of how far fingers can be spread apart.

apex In a pyramid or a cone, the vertex opposite the base.

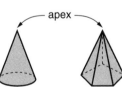

arc Part of a circle, from one point on the circle to another. For example, a *semicircle* is an arc whose endpoints are the endpoints of a diameter of the circle.

area The amount of surface inside a closed boundary. Area is measured in square units, such as square inches or square centimeters.

area model A model for multiplication problems in which the length and width of a rectangle represent the factors and the area of the rectangle represents the product. Also, a model for showing fractions as parts of circles, rectangles, or other geometric figures.

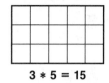

$3 * 5 = 15$

array An arrangement of objects in a regular pattern, usually rows and columns. Arrays can be used to model multiplication. For example, the array below is a model for $3 * 5 = 15$.

associative property A property of addition and multiplication (but not of subtraction or division) that says when you add or multiply three numbers, it doesn't matter which two are added or multiplied first. For example:

(4 + 3) + 7 = 4 + (3 + 7) and
(5 * 8) * 9 = 5 * (8 * 9).

average A typical value for a set of numbers. The word *average* usually refers to the *mean* of a set of numbers, but there are other averages. See also *mean*, *median*, and *mode*.

axis (1) Either of the two number lines that intersect to form a *coordinate grid*. (2) A line about which a solid figure rotates.

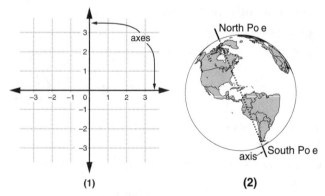

(1)   (2)

base (in exponential notation) The number that is raised to some power. For example, in 5^3, the base is 5. See also *exponential notation*.

base-ten The feature of our number system that results in each place having a value 10 times the place to its right. See also *place value*.

billion 1,000,000,000, or 10^9.

bisect To divide a segment, an angle, or a figure into two equal parts.

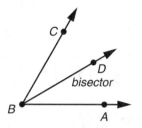

Ray *BD* bisects Angle *ABC*.

cell In a spreadsheet, a box formed where a column and a row intersect. A column is a section of cells lined up vertically. A row is a section of cells lined up horizontally.

centimeter (cm) In the metric system, a unit of length equivalent to $\frac{1}{100}$ of a meter; 10 millimeters; $\frac{1}{10}$ of a decimeter.

circle The set of all points in a plane that are a given distance from a given point in the plane. The given point is the *center* of the circle, and the given distance is the *radius*.

circle graph A graph in which a circle and its interior are divided into parts to show the parts of a set of data. The whole circle represents the whole set of data. Same as *pie graph*.

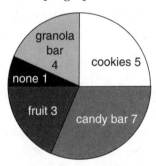

circumference The distance around a circle or a sphere; the perimeter of a circle.

column-addition method A method for adding numbers in which the addends' digits are first added in each place-value column separately and then 10-for-1 trades are made until each column has only one digit. Lines are drawn to separate the place-value columns.

column-division method A division procedure in which vertical lines are drawn between the digits of the dividend. The lines make the procedure easier to carry out.

common denominator Any number, except zero, that is a multiple of the denominators of two or more fractions. For example, the fractions $\frac{1}{2}$ and $\frac{2}{3}$ have the common denominators 6, 12, 18, and so on. See also *denominator*.

common factor Any number that is a factor of two or more numbers. For example, 4 is a common factor of 8 and 12.

commutative property A property of addition and multiplication (but not of subtraction or division) that says that changing the order of the numbers being added or multiplied doesn't change the answer. For example: $5 + 10 = 10 + 5$ and $3 * 8 = 8 * 3$.

complementary angles Two angles whose measures total 90°.

Angles 1 and 2 are complementary angles.

composite number A whole number that has more than two factors. For example, 4 is a composite number because it has three factors: 1, 2, and 4.

concave polygon A polygon in which at least one vertex is "pushed in." Not every line segment with endpoints on a concave polygon is entirely inside the polygon. Same as *nonconvex polygon*.

concentric circles Circles that have the same center but radii of different lengths.

cone A 3-dimensional shape that has a circular *base*, a curved surface, and one vertex, which is called the *apex*. The points on the curved surface of a cone are on straight lines connecting the apex and the circumference of the base.

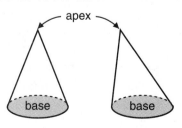

congruent Having exactly the same shape and size.

consecutive angles Two angles in a polygon that share a common side.

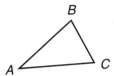

Angles *A* and *B*, *B* and *C*, and *C* and *A* are pairs of consecutive angles.

convex polygon A polygon in which all vertices are "pushed outward." Any line segment with endpoints on a convex polygon lies entirely inside the polygon.

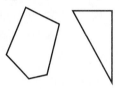

coordinate grid A device for locating points in a plane using *ordered numbered pairs*, or coordinates. A *rectangular coordinate grid* is formed by two number lines that intersect at right angles at their zero points. See also *ordered number pair*.

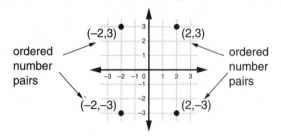

rectangular coordinate grid

corresponding Having the same relative position in *similar* or *congruent figures*. In the diagram, pairs of corresponding sides are marked with the same number of slash marks.

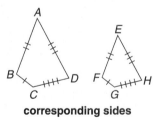

corresponding sides

cross multiplication The process of finding the cross products of two fractions. Cross multiplication can be used in solving proportions.

$$\frac{3}{4} = \frac{z}{20}$$

$4 * z = 4z$

$3 * 20 = 60$

cube A polyhedron with 6 square faces. A cube has 8 vertices and 12 edges.

cubic centimeter A metric unit of volume equal to the volume of a cube that is 1 cm on each side. 1 cubic centimeter is equal to 1 milliliter.

cubic unit A unit used in measuring volume, such as cubic centimeters or cubic feet.

cylinder A 3-dimensional shape that has two circular or elliptical bases that are parallel and congruent and are connected by a curved surface. The points on the curved surface of a cylinder are on straight lines connecting corresponding points on the bases. A can is shaped like a cylinder.

decennial Occurring or being done every 10 years.

decimal A number that contains a decimal point, such as 2.54. See also *standard notation*.

decimal point A dot used to separate the ones and tenths places in decimal numbers.

decimeter (dm) In the metric system, a unit of length equivalent to $\frac{1}{10}$ of a meter; 10 centimeters.

deficient number A number whose proper factors add up to less than the number itself. For example, 10 is a deficient number because the sum of its proper factors is $1 + 2 + 5 = 8$, and 8 is less than 10. See also *proper factor* and *perfect number*.

degree (°) A unit of measure for angles based on dividing a circle into 360 equal parts. Also, a unit of measure for temperature. A small raised circle (°) is used to show degrees.

denominator The number below the line in a fraction. In a fraction where a whole is divided into equal parts, the denominator represents the number of equal parts into which the whole (the ONE or unit) is divided. In the fraction $\frac{a}{b}$, b is the denominator.

density A *rate* that compares the *mass* of an object with its *volume*. For example, suppose a ball has a mass of 20 grams and a volume of 10 cubic centimeters. To find its density, divide its mass by its volume: $20 \text{ g}/10 \text{ cm}^3 = 2 \text{ g/cm}^3$, or 2 grams per cubic centimeter.

diameter A line segment that passes through the center of a circle or sphere and has endpoints on the circle or sphere; also, the length of this line segment. The diameter of a circle or sphere is twice the length of its radius.

difference The result of subtracting one number from another.

digit One of the number symbols 0, 1, 2, 3, 4, 5, 6, 7, 8, 9.

distributive property A property that relates multiplication and addition or subtraction. This property gets its name because it "distributes" a factor over terms inside parentheses.

Distributive property of multiplication over addition:
$a * (b + c) = (a * b) + (a * c)$, so
$2 * (5 + 3) = (2 * 5) + (2 * 3) = 10 + 6 = 16$

Distributive property of multiplication over subtraction:
$a * (b - c) = (a * b) - (a * c)$
$2 * (5 - 3) = (2 * 5) - (2 * 3) = 10 - 6 = 4$

dividend The number in division that is being divided. For example, in $35 \div 5 = 7$, the dividend is 35.

divisibility test A test to find out whether a whole number is *divisible by* another whole number without actually doing the division. A divisibility test for 5, for example, is to check the last digit: if the last digit is 0 or 5, then the number is divisible by 5.

divisible by One whole number is divisible by another whole number if there is no remainder when you divide. For example, 28 is divisible by 7 because 28 divided by 7 is 4 with a remainder of 0.

Division of Fractions Property The principle that says that division by a fraction is equivalent to multiplication by that fraction's *reciprocal*. For example, since the *reciprocal* of $\frac{1}{2}$ is 2, the division problem $4 \div \frac{1}{2}$ is equivalent to the multiplication problem $4 * 2$.

divisor In division, the number that divides another number. For example, in $35 \div 5 = 7$, the divisor is 5.

edge A line segment where two faces of a polyhedron meet.

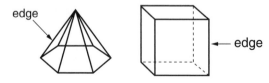

endpoint A point at the end of a line segment or ray. A line segment is normally named using the letter labels of its endpoints. See *line segment* and *ray*.

equation A number sentence that contains an equal sign. For example, $15 = 10 + 5$ is an equation.

equilateral triangle A triangle with all three sides equal in length and all three angles having the same measure.

equivalent Equal in value but possibly in a different form. For example, $\frac{1}{2}$, 0.5, and 50% are all equivalent.

equivalent equations Equations that have the same solution. For example, $2 + x = 4$ and $6 + x = 8$ are equivalent equations because the solution to both is $x = 2$.

equivalent fractions Fractions that have different denominators but name the same amount. For example, $\frac{1}{2}$ and $\frac{4}{8}$ are equivalent fractions.

equivalent rates *Rates* that make the same comparison. For example, the rates $\frac{60 \text{ miles}}{1 \text{ hour}}$ and $\frac{1 \text{ mile}}{1 \text{ minute}}$ are equivalent.

equivalent ratios *Ratios* that make the same comparison. Equivalent ratios can be expressed by *equivalent fractions*. For example, the ratios 12 to 20, 6 to 10, and 3 to 5 are equivalent ratios because $\frac{12}{20} = \frac{6}{10} = \frac{3}{5}$.

exponent A small raised number in *exponential notation* that tells how many times the base is to be multiplied by itself. For example, in 5^3, the exponent is 3. See also *base* and *exponential notation*.

exponential notation A way to show repeated multiplication by the same factor. For example, 2^3 is exponential notation for $2 * 2 * 2$. The small raised 3 is the exponent. It tells how many times the number 2, called the base, is used as a factor.

expression A group of mathematical symbols that represents a number—or can represent a number if values are assigned to any variables in the expression.

extended multiplication fact A multiplication fact involving multiples of 10, 100, and so on. In an extended multiplication fact, each factor has only one digit that is not 0. For example, $6 * 70$, $60 * 7$, and $60 * 70$ are extended multiplication facts.

face A flat surface on a 3-dimensional shape.

fact family A set of related addition and subtraction facts or related multiplication and division facts. For example, $5 + 6 = 11$, $6 + 5 = 11$, $11 - 5 = 6$, and $11 - 6 = 5$ are a fact family. $5 * 7 = 35$, $7 * 5 = 35$, $35 \div 5 = 7$, and $35 \div 7 = 5$ are another fact family.

factor One of two or more numbers that are multiplied to give a product. The numbers that are multiplied are called *factors* of the product. For example, 4 and 3 are factors of 12 because $4 * 3 = 12$. As a verb, *to factor* means to find two (or more) smaller numbers whose product equals a given number. 15, for example, can be factored as $5 * 3$.

factor pair Two whole-number factors of a number whose product is the number. A number may have more than one factor pair. For example, the factor pairs for 18 are 1 and 18, 2 and 9, and 3 and 6.

factor rainbow A way to show factor pairs in a list of all the factors of a number. A factor rainbow can be used to check whether a list of factors is correct.

factor rainbow for 24

factor string A number written as a product of at least two whole-number factors. For example, a factor string for the number 24 is $2 * 3 * 4$. This factor string has three factors, so its length is 3. The number 1 is never part of a factor string.

factor tree A way to get the *prime factorization* of a number. The original number is written as a product of factors; then each of these factors is written as a product of factors, and so on, until the factors are all prime numbers. A factor tree looks like an upside down tree, with the root (the original number) at the top and the leaves (the factors) beneath it. See *prime factorization*.

factorial A product of a whole number and all the smaller whole numbers except 0. An exclamation point, !, is used to write factorials. For example, "three factorial" is written as 3! and is equal to $3 * 2 * 1 = 6$. $10! = 10 * 9 * 8 * 7 * 6 * 5 * 4 * 3 * 2 * 1 = 3,628,800$.

figurate numbers Numbers that can be shown by specific geometric patterns. Square numbers and triangular numbers are examples of figurate numbers.

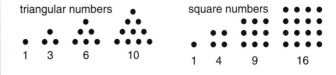

flip See *reflection*.

formula A general rule for finding the value of something. A formula is often written using letters, called variables, that stand for the quantities involved. For example, the formula for the area of a rectangle may be written as $A = l * w$, where A represents the area of the rectangle, l represents its length, and w represents its width.

fraction stick A diagram used in *Everyday Mathematics* to represent simple fractions.

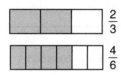

fulcrum A point on a mobile at which a rod is suspended. In general, the point or place around which a lever pivots.

general pattern A model or plan by which elements can be arranged so that what comes next can be predicted.

geometric solid A 3-dimensional shape, such as a prism, pyramid, cylinder, cone, or sphere. Despite its name, a geometric solid is hollow; it does not contain the points in its interior.

Golden Rectangle A rectangle in which the ratio of the length of the longer side to the length of the shorter side is the Golden Ratio, or about 1.618 to 1. A 5-inch by 3-inch index card is nearly a Golden Rectangle.

greatest common factor The largest factor that two or more numbers have in common. For example, the common factors of 24 and 36 are 1, 2, 3, 4, 6, and 12; the greatest common factor of 24 and 36 is 12.

grouping symbols Symbols such as parentheses ( ), brackets [ ], and braces { } that tell the order in which operations in an expression are to be done. For example, in the expression (3 + 4) * 5, you should do the operation in the parentheses first. The expression then becomes 7 * 5 = 35.

hemisphere Half of Earth's surface. Also, half of a sphere.

heptagon A polygon with seven sides.

hexagon A polygon with six sides.

hexagram A 6-pointed star formed by extending the sides of a regular hexagon.

horizon Where the earth and sky appear to meet; if nothing is in the way, as when looking out to sea, the horizon looks like a line.

hundredths The place-value position in which a digit has a value equal to $\frac{1}{100}$ of itself; the second digit to the right of the decimal point.

hypotenuse In a right triangle, the side opposite the right angle.

image The reflection of an object that you see when you look in a mirror. Also, a figure that is produced by a transformation (a reflection, translation, or rotation, for example) of another figure. See also *preimage*.

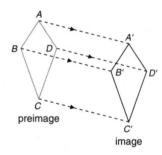

improper fraction A fraction whose numerator is greater than or equal to its denominator. For example, $\frac{4}{3}$, $\frac{5}{2}$, $\frac{4}{4}$, and $\frac{24}{12}$ are improper fractions. In *Everyday Mathematics*, improper fractions are sometimes called "top-heavy" fractions.

indirect measurement Methods for determining heights, distances, and other quantities that cannot be measured directly.

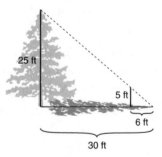

inequality A number sentence with >, <, ≥, ≤, or ≠. For example, the sentence 8 < 15 is an inequality.

inscribed polygon A polygon whose vertices are all on the same circle.

inscribed square

integer A number in the set {..., -4, -3, -2, -1, 0, 1, 2, 3, 4, ...}; a *whole number* or the *opposite* of a whole number.

intersecting Meeting or crossing one another. Lines, segments, rays, and planes can intersect.

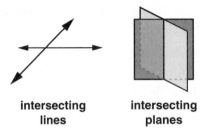

intersecting lines   intersecting planes

interval (1) The set of numbers between two numbers *a* and *b*, which may include *a* or *b* or both. (2) A part of a line, including all points between two specific points.

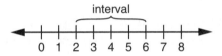

irrational number A number that cannot be written as a fraction where both the numerator and denominator are *integers* and the denominator is not zero. For example, π is an irrational number.

isometry transformation A transformation such as a *translation* (slide), *reflection* (flip), or *rotation* (turn) that changes the position or orientation of a figure but does not change its size or shape.

slide   flip   turn

isosceles triangle A triangle with at least two sides that are the same length. In an isosceles triangle, at least two angles have the same measure.

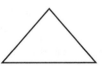

kite A quadrilateral with two pairs of adjacent equal sides. The four sides cannot all have the same length, so a rhombus is not a kite.

landmark A notable feature of a data set. Landmarks include the *mean, median, mode, maximum, minimum,* and *range.*

lattice method A very old way to multiply multidigit numbers.

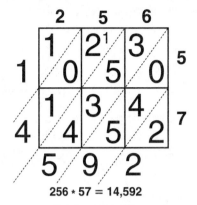

$256 * 57 = 14,592$

least common denominator The *least common multiple* of the denominators of every fraction in a given collection. For example, the least common denominator of $\frac{1}{2}$, $\frac{4}{5}$, and $\frac{3}{8}$ is 40. See also *least common multiple.*

least common multiple The smallest number that is a multiple of two or more numbers. For example, while some common multiples of 6 and 8 are 24, 48, and 72, the least common multiple of 6 and 8 is 24.

left-to-right subtraction A subtraction method in which you start at the left and subtract column by column.

leg of a right triangle A side of a right triangle that is not the *hypotenuse.* See also *hypotenuse.*

like terms In an *algebraic expression,* either the constant terms or any terms that contain the same variable(s) raised to the same power(s). For example, $4y$ and $7y$ are like terms in the expression $4y + 7y - z$.

line A straight path that extends infinitely in opposite directions.

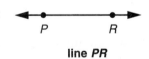

line *PR*

line graph A graph in which data points are connected by line segments.

line of reflection (mirror line) A line halfway between a figure (preimage) and its reflected image. In a reflection, a figure is "flipped over" the line of reflection. See also *reflection.*

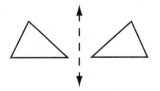

line of symmetry A line drawn through a figure that divides it into two parts that look exactly alike but are facing in opposite directions. See also *line symmetry*.

line of symmetry

line plot A sketch of data in which check marks, Xs, or other marks above a labeled line show the frequency of each value.

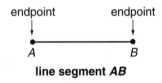

line segment A straight path joining two points. The two points are called the *endpoints* of the segment.

endpoint   endpoint

A   B

line segment *AB*

line symmetry A figure has line symmetry if a line can be drawn through it so that it is divided into two parts with both parts looking exactly alike but facing in opposite directions. See also *line of symmetry*.

lowest terms See *simplest form*.

magnitude estimate A very rough estimate. A magnitude estimate tells whether an answer should be in the tens, hundreds, thousands, millions, and so on.

mean The sum of a set of numbers divided by the number of numbers in the set. The mean is often referred to simply as the *average*.

median The middle value in a set of data when the data are listed in order from smallest to largest. If there is an even number of data points, the median is the *mean* of the two middle values.

meter (m) In the metric system, the fundamental unit of length from which other units of length are derived. One meter is the distance light will travel in a vacuum (empty space) in $\frac{1}{299,792,458}$ second.

metric system of measurement A measurement system based on the base-ten numeration system. It is used in most countries around the world.

millimeter (mm) In the metric system, a unit of length equivalent to $\frac{1}{1,000}$ of a meter; $\frac{1}{10}$ of a centimeter.

million 1,000,000, or 10^6.

minuend The number that is reduced in subtraction. For example, in 19 − 5 = 14, the minuend is 19.

mixed number A number that is written using both a whole number and a fraction. For example, $2\frac{1}{4}$ is a mixed number equal to $2 + \frac{1}{4}$.

mode The value or values that occur most often in a set of data.

multiple of a number *n* (1) A product of *n* and a counting number. The multiples of 7, for example, are 7, 14, 21, 28, … (2) A product of *n* and an integer. The multiples of 7, for example, are …, -21, -14, -7, 0, 7, 14, 21, …

multiplication diagram A diagram used for problems in which there are several equal groups. The diagram has three parts: a number of groups, a number in each group, and a total number. Also called *multiplication/division diagram*.

multiplication property of −1 A property of multiplication that says that for any number *a*, (−1) ∗ *a* = (op) *a*, or −*a*. For example, for *a* = 5: 5 ∗ (−1) = (op) 5 = −5. For *a* = −3: −3 ∗ (−1) = (op) −3 = −(−3) = 3.

multiplicative inverses Two numbers whose product is 1. For example, the multiplicative inverse of 5 is $\frac{1}{5}$, and the multiplicative inverse of $\frac{3}{5}$ is $\frac{5}{3}$. Multiplicative inverses are also called *reciprocals* of each other.

name-collection box A diagram that is used for writing equivalent names for a number.

negative number A number that is less than zero; a number to the left of zero on a horizontal number line or below zero on a vertical number line.

nested parentheses Parentheses inside parentheses. For example, ((6 ∗ 4) − 2) ÷ 2 = (24 − 2) ÷ 2 = 22 ÷ 2 = 11

***n*-gon** A polygon with *n* sides. For example, a 5-gon is a pentagon, and an 8-gon is an octagon.

***n*-to-1 ratio** A ratio of a number to 1. Every ratio can be converted to an *n*-to-1 ratio. For example, to convert the ratio of 3 girls to 2 boys to an *n*-to-1 ratio, divide 3 by 2. The *n*-to-1 ratio is 1.5 to 1.

nonconvex polygon See *concave polygon*.

number-and-word notation A way of writing a large number using a combination of numbers and words. For example, *27 billion* is number-and-word notation for 27,000,000,000.

number sentence At least two numbers or expressions separated by a relation symbol (=, >, <, ≥, ≥, ≠). Most number sentences contain at least one operation symbol (+, −, ×, *, •, ÷, /). Number sentences may also have grouping symbols, such as parentheses.

numerator The number above the line in a fraction. In a fraction where a whole is divided into equal parts, the numerator represents the number of equal parts being considered. In the fraction $\frac{a}{b}$, a is the numerator.

100% box The entire object, the entire collection of objects, or the entire quantity being considered.

ones The place-value position in which a digit has a value equal to the digit itself.

open sentence A *number sentence* in which one or more *variables* hold the places of missing numbers. An open sentence is neither true nor false. For example, $5 + x = 13$ is an open sentence. See also *number sentence* and *variable*.

operation symbol A symbol used to stand for a particular mathematical operation. The most widely used operation symbols are +, −, ×, *, •, ÷, and /.

opposite angles (1) of a *quadrilateral*: Angles that do not share a common side.

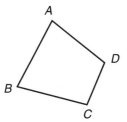

**Angles *A* and *C* and Angles *B* and *D*
are pairs of opposite angles.**

(2) of a *triangle*: An angle is opposite the side of a triangle that is not one of the sides of the angle.

(3) of two lines that *intersect*: The angles that do not share a common

Angle *C* is opposite side *AB*.

side are opposite angles. Opposite angles have equal measures. See also *vertical angles*.

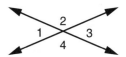

**Angles 2 and 4 and Angles 1 and 3 are pairs
of opposite, or vertical, angles.**

opposite of a number A number that is the same distance from 0 on the number line as a given number but on the opposite side of 0. For example, the opposite of +3 is −3, and the opposite of −5 is +5.

order of operations Rules that tell in what order to perform operations in arithmetic and algebra.
1. Do the operations in parentheses first. (Use rules 2–4 inside the parentheses.)
2. Calculate all the expressions with exponents.
3. Multiply and divide in order from left to right.
4. Add and subtract in order from left to right.

ordered number pair Two numbers that are used to locate a point on a *coordinate grid*. The first number gives the position along the horizontal axis, and the second number gives the position along the vertical axis. The numbers in an ordered pair are called coordinates. Ordered pairs are usually written inside parentheses: (5,3). See also *coordinate grid*.

origin The 0 point on a number line or in a coordinate grid.

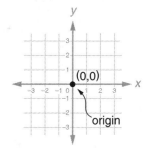

outcome A possible result of a random process. For example, heads and tails are the two possible outcomes of tossing a coin.

parabola The curve formed by the intersection of a right circular cone with a plane that is parallel to a line on the cone.

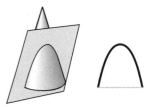

parallel Never meeting and always the same distance apart. Lines, line segments, rays, and planes are parallel if they never meet, no matter how far they are extended. The symbol ∥ means "is parallel to."

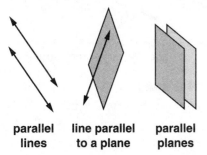

parallel   line parallel   parallel
lines   to a plane   planes

parallelogram A quadrilateral with two pairs of parallel sides. Opposite sides of a parallelogram are congruent.

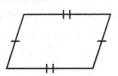

parentheses Grouping symbols, ( ), used to tell which parts of an expression should be calculated first.

partial-differences method A way to subtract in which differences are computed for each place (one, tens, hundreds, and so on) separately. The partial differences are then added to give the final answer.

	932
	− 356
1. Subtract 100s: 900 − 300.	600
2. Subtract 10s: 30 − 50.	− 20
3. Subtract 1s: 2 − 6.	− 4
4. Add the partial differences.	576
(600 − 20 − 4, done mentally)	

partial-products method A way to multiply in which the value of each digit in one factor is multiplied by the value of each digit in the other factor. The final product is the sum of the several partial products.

	67
	× 53
50 × 60	3,000
50 × 7	350
3 × 60	180
3 × 7	+ 21
	3,551

partial-quotients method A way to divide in which the dividend is divided in a series of steps and the quotients for each step (called partial quotients) are added to give the final answer.

partial-sums method A way to add in which sums are computed for each place (ones, tens, hundreds, and so on) separately and are then added to give the final answer.

	268
	+ 483
1. Add 100s.	600
2. Adds 10s.	140
3. Add 1s.	+ 11
4. Add the partial sums.	751

part-to-part ratio A ratio that compares a part of a whole to another part of the same whole. For example, the statement "There are 8 boys for every 12 girls" expresses a part-to-part ratio. See also *ratio* and *part-to-whole ratio*.

part-to-whole ratio A *ratio* that compares a part of a whole to the whole. For example, the statements "8 out of 20 students are boys" and "12 out of 20 students are girls" both express part-to-whole ratios. See also *ratio* and *part-to-part ratio*.

per-unit rate A *rate* with 1 in the denominator.

percent (%) Per hundred or out of a hundred. For example, "48% of the students in the school are boys" means that 48 out of every 100 students in the school are boys.

Percent Circle A tool on the *Geometry Template* that is used to measure and draw figures that involve percents (such as circle graphs).

percent or fraction of a discount The percent or fraction that tells what part of the regular price you save.

perfect number A number whose *proper factors* add up to the number itself. For example, 6 is a perfect number because the sum of its proper factors is 1 + 2 + 3 = 6. See also *proper factor* and *deficient number*.

perimeter The distance around a closed 2-dimensional shape. A formula for the perimeter of a rectangle is $P = 2 * (l + w)$, where l represents the length and w represents the width of the rectangle.

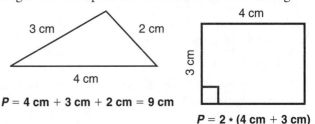

$P = 4\ cm + 3\ cm + 2\ cm = 9\ cm$

$P = 2 * (4\ cm + 3\ cm)$

perpendicular Meeting at right angles. Lines, rays, line segments, and planes that meet at right angles are perpendicular. The symbol ⊥ means "is perpendicular to."

personal measurement reference A convenient approximation for a standard unit of measurement. For example, many people have thumbs that are 1 inch wide.

perspective drawing A method of drawing that realistically represents a 3-dimensional object on a 2-dimensional surface.

per-unit rate A *rate* with 1 in the denominator. Per-unit rates tell how many of one thing there are for one of another thing. For example, "2 dollars per gallon" is a per-gallon rate. "12 miles per hour" and "4 words per minute" are also examples of per-unit rates.

pi (π) The ratio of the *circumference* of a circle to its *diameter*. Pi is also the ratio of the area of a circle to the square of its radius. Pi is the same for every circle and is an irrational number that is approximately equal to 3.14.

pie graph See *circle graph*.

place value A system that values a digit according to its position in a number. In our number system, each place has a value that is ten times that of the place to its right and one-tenth the value of the place to its left. For example, in the number 456, the 4 is in the hundreds place and has a value of 400.

plane A flat surface that extends forever.

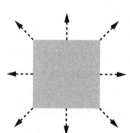

point symmetry The property of balance in a figure that can be rotated 180° about a point in such a way that the resulting figure (the *image*) exactly matches the original figure (the *preimage*). Point symmetry is *rotation symmetry* in which the turn is 180°. See also *rotation symmetry*.

rotational symmetry

polygon A closed 2-dimensional figure that is made up of line segments joined end to end. The line segments of a polygon may not cross.

polyhedron A closed 3-dimensional figure whose surfaces, or faces, are all formed by polygons and their interiors.

power of 10 A whole number that can be written using only 10s as factors. For example, 100 is equal to 10 * 10, or 10^2. 100 can be called the second power of 10 or 10 to the second power. Negative powers of 10 are numbers that can be written using only $\frac{1}{10}$ as a factor.

precision A measure of how exactly a count or measurement was determined and how reliable or repeatable the result is; a measure of the uncertainty of a result. For example, if several people counted the same things or measured the same object, to what extent would their results agree? The precision of a measurement may be improved by using measuring instruments with smaller units.

predict To tell what will happen ahead of time; to make an educated guess about what might happen.

preimage A geometric figure that is somehow changed (by a *reflection*, *rotation*, or *translation*, for example) to produce another figure. See also *image*.

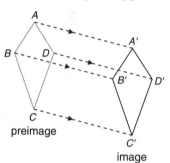

preimage   image

prime factorization A whole number expressed as a product of prime factors. Every composite number has a unique prime factorization. For example, the prime factorization of 24 is 2 * 2 * 2 * 3.

prime number A whole number that has exactly two *factors*: itself and 1. For example, 5 is a prime number because its only factors are 5 and 1.

prism A solid with two parallel *faces*, called *bases*, that are congruent polygons and its other *faces* that are all parallelograms. The points on the lateral faces of a prism are all on lines connecting corresponding points on the bases. Prisms get their names from the shape of their bases.

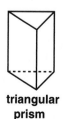 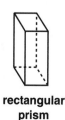 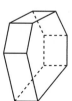

triangular prism   **rectangular prism**   **hexagonal prism**

probability A number from 0 to 1 that tells the chance that an event will happen. The closer a probability is to 1, the more likely the event is to happen.

probability tree diagram A drawing used to analyze the possible outcomes in a random situation. For example, the "leaves" of the probability tree diagram below represent the four equally likely outcomes when one coin is flipped two times.

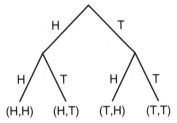

product The result of multiplying two numbers called *factors*. For example, in 4 * 3 = 12, the product is 12.

proper factor Any whole-number *factor* of a number except the number itself. For example, the *factors* of 10 are 1, 2, 5, and 10, but the *proper factors* of 10 are 1, 2, and 5.

proper fraction A fraction in which the numerator is less than the denominator; a proper fraction names a number that is less than 1. For example, $\frac{3}{4}$, $\frac{2}{5}$, and $\frac{12}{24}$ are proper fractions.

proportion A number model that states that two fractions are equal. Often the fractions in a proportion represent rates or ratios. For example, the problem *Alan's speed is 12 miles per hour. At the same speed, how far can he travel in 3 hours?* can be modeled by the proportion $\frac{12 \text{ miles}}{1 \text{ hour}} = \frac{n \text{ miles}}{3 \text{ hours}}$.

protractor A tool for measuring and drawing angles. A half-circle protractor can be used to measure and draw angles up to 180°; a full-circle protractor, to measure and draw angles up to 360°.

pyramid A solid in which one face, the *base*, is any polygon and all the other *faces* are triangles that come together at a point called the *vertex*, or *apex*. Pyramids get their names from the shape of their bases.

 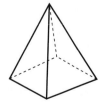

hexagonal pyramid   **rectangular pyramid**

Pythagorean theorem The following famous theorem: If the *legs of a right triangle* have lengths *a* and *b* and the hypotenuse has length *c*, then $a^2 + b^2 = c^2$.

quick common denominator The product of the denominators of two or more fractions. For example, the quick common denominator of $\frac{1}{4}$ and $\frac{3}{6}$ is 4 * 6, or 24. As the name suggests, this is a quick way to get a *common denominator* for a collection of fractions, but it does not necessarily give the *least common denominator*.

quotient The result of dividing one number by another number. For example, in 35 ÷ 5 = 7, the quotient is 7.

radius A line segment from the center of a circle (or sphere) to any point on the circle (or sphere); also, the length of such a line segment.

random number A number that has the same chance of appearing as any other number. Rolling a fair die will produce random numbers.

range The difference between the maximum and the minimum in a set of data.

rate A comparison by division of two quantities with unlike units. For example, a speed such as 55 miles per hour is a rate that compares distance with time. See also *ratio*.

ratio A comparison by division of two quantities with like units. Ratios can be expressed with fractions, decimals, percents, or words. Sometimes they are written with a colon between the two numbers that are being compared. For example, if a team wins 3 games out of 5 games played, the ratio of wins to total games can be written as $\frac{3}{5}$, 0.6, 60%, 3 to 5, or 3:5. See also *rate*.

rational number A number that can be written as a fraction using only whole numbers and their opposites.

ray A straight path that extends infinitely from a point called its *endpoint*.

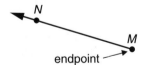

endpoint

real number Any *rational* or *irrational number*.

reciprocal Same as *multiplicative inverse*.

rectangular method A method for finding area in which rectangles are drawn around a figure or parts of a figure. The rectangles form regions that are rectangles or triangular halves of rectangles. The area of the original figure can be found by adding or subtracting the areas of these regions.

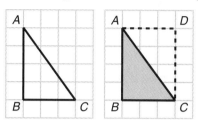

rectangular prism A *prism* with rectangular bases. See also *prism*.

reflection The "flipping" of a figure over a line (the *line of reflection*) so that its image is the mirror image of the original. A reflection of a solid figure is a "flip" over a plane. Same as *flip*.

regular polygon A polygon whose sides are all the same length and whose angles are all equal.

regular polyhedron A polyhedron whose faces are formed by a single kind of congruent *regular polygon* and in which every vertex looks exactly the same as every other vertex. There are five regular polyhedrons:

tetrahedron   cube   octahedron

dodecahedron   icosahedron

relation symbol A symbol used to express a relationship between two quantities.

= for "is equal to" ≠ for "is not equal to"
> for "is greater than" < for "is less than"
≥ for "is greater than or equal to"
≤ for "is less than or equal to"

remainder An amount left over when one number is divided by another number. For example, if you divide 38 by 5, you get 7 equal groups with a remainder of 3. We may write 38 ÷ 5 → 7 R3, where R3 stands for the remainder.

repeating decimal A *decimal* in which one digit or a group of digits is repeated without end. For example, 0.3333... and 0.$\overline{147}$ are repeating decimals. See also *decimal* and *terminating decimal*.

rhombus A quadrilateral whose sides are all the same length.

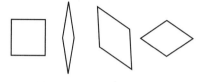

right prism or cylinder A prism or cylinder whose bases are perpendicular to its other faces or surfaces.

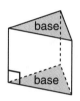

right pyramid or cone A pyramid or cone whose apex is directly above the center of its base.

right triangle A triangle that has a right angle.

rotation A movement of a figure around a fixed point, or axis; a *"turn."*

rotation symmetry A figure has rotation symmetry if it can be rotated less than a full turn around a point or an axis so that the resulting figure (the *image*) exactly matches the original figure (the *preimage*).

round To adjust a number to make it easier to work with or to make it better reflect the level of precision of the data. Often numbers are rounded to the nearest multiple of 10, 100, 1,000, and so on. For example, 12,964 rounded to the nearest thousand is 13,000.

scale The *ratio* of a distance on a map, globe, drawing, or model to an actual distance.

scale drawing A drawing of an object or a region in which all parts are drawn to the same *scale*. Architects and builders often use scale drawings.

scale factor The *ratio* between the size of an object and the size of a drawing or model of that object (such as a *scale drawing* or a *scale model*).

scale model A model of an object in which all parts are in the same proportions as in the actual object. For example, many model trains and airplanes are scale models of actual vehicles.

scalene triangle A triangle with sides of three different lengths. In a scalene triangle, all three angles have different measures.

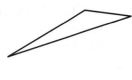

scientific notation A system for writing numbers in which a number is written as the product of a *power of 10* and a number that is at least 1 and less than 10. Scientific notation allows you to write big and small numbers with only a few symbols. For example, 4 * 10^{12} is scientific notation for 4,000,000,000,000.

sector A region bounded by an *arc* and two *radii* of a circle. A sector resembles a slice of pizza. The word *wedge* is sometimes used instead of sector.

side One of the line segments that make up a polygon.

significant digits The *digits* in a number that convey useful and reliable information. A number with more significant digits is more *precise* than a number with fewer significant digits.

similar Exactly the same shape but not necessarily the same size.

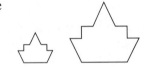

similar figures

simpler form A fraction can be put in simpler form by dividing its numerator and denominator by a whole number that is greater than 1. For example, $\frac{18}{24}$ can be put in simpler form by dividing the numerator and denominator by 2. The result, $\frac{9}{12}$, is in simpler form than $\frac{18}{24}$.

simplest form A fraction less than 1 is in simplest form if there is no number other than 1 that divides its numerator and denominator evenly. A *mixed number* is in simplest form if its fractional part is in simplest form.

simplify (1) of a fraction: To express in *simpler form*. (2) of an equation or expression: To rewrite by removing parentheses and combining like terms and constants. For example, $7y + 4 + 5 + 3y$ can be simplified as $10y + 9$, and $2(a + 4) = 4a + 1 + 3$ can be simplified as $2a + 8 = 4a + 4$.

simulation A model of a real situation. For example, a fair coin can be used to simulate a series of games between two equally matched teams.

size-change factor A number that tells the amount of enlargement or reduction.

skew lines Lines in space that do not lie in the same plane. Skew lines do not *intersect* and are not *parallel*. For example, an east-west line on the floor and a north-south line on the ceiling are skew.

slanted prism or cylinder A prism or cylinder whose bases are not perpendicular to all of its other faces or surfaces.

slanted pyramid or cone A pyramid or cone whose apex is not directly above the center of its base.

slide See *translation*.

solution set The set of all solutions of an equation or inequality. For example, the solution set of $x^2 = 25$ is {5, -5} since substitution of either 5 or –5 for *x* makes the sentence true.

special case (of a pattern) An instance when values replace the words or variables in a general pattern. For example, $6 + 6 = 12$ is a special case of the pattern $Y + Y = 2Y$.

speed A rate that compares a distance traveled with the time taken to travel that distance. For example, if you went 100 miles in 2 hours, your speed was 100 mi / 2 hr, or 50 miles per hour.

sphere The set of all points in space that are a given distance from a given point. The given point is the center of the sphere, and the given distance is the radius.

square A rectangle with all sides equal.

square number A number that is the product of a whole number multiplied by itself. For example, 25 is a square number because $25 = 5 * 5$. The square numbers are 1, 4, 9, 16, 25, and so on.

square of a number The product of a number multiplied by itself. For example, 81 is the square of 9 because $81 = 9 * 9$.

square root of a number The square root of a number *n* is a number that, when multiplied by itself, gives the number *n*. For example, 4 is the square root of 16 because $4 * 4 = 16$.

square unit A unit used in measuring area, such as square centimeters or square feet.

standard notation The most familiar way of representing whole numbers, integers, and decimals. In standard notation, the value of each digit depends on where the digit is. For example, standard notation for three hundred fifty-six is 356. See also *place value*.

stem-and-leaf plot A display of data in which digits with larger *place values* are "stems" and digits with smaller *place values* are "leaves."

subtrahend In subtraction, the number that is being taken away from another number. For example, in $19 - 5 = 14$, the subtrahend is 5.

sum The result of adding two or more numbers. For example, in $5 + 3 = 8$, the sum is 8.

supplementary angles Two angles whose measures total 180°.

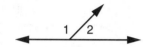

Angles 1 and 2 are supplementary angles.

surface (1) The outside boundary of an object; the part of an object that is next to the air. Common surfaces include the top of a body of water, the outermost part of a ball, and the topmost layer of ground that covers Earth. (2) Any 2-dimensional layer, such as a plane or the faces of a polyhedron.

surface area A measure of the surface of a 3-dimensional figure.

symmetric Having the same size and shape on either side of a line or looking the same when turned by some amount less than 360°. See also *line symmetry*, *point symmetry*, and *rotation symmetry*.

tens The place-value position in which a digit has a value equal to ten times itself.

tenths The place-value position in which a digit has a value equal to $\frac{1}{10}$ of itself; the first digit to the right of the decimal point.

term In an *algebraic expression*, a number or a product of a number and one or more variables. For example, in the expression $5y + 3k - 8$, the terms are $5y$, $3k$, and 8.

terminating decimal A decimal that ends. For example, 0.5 and 0.125 are terminating decimals. See also *decimal* and *repeating decimal*.

tessellation An arrangement of shapes that covers a surface completely without overlaps or gaps. Also called a *tiling*.

test number A number used to replace a variable when solving an equation using the *trial-and-error method*. Test numbers are useful for "closing in" on an exact solution. See also *trial-and-error method*.

tetrahedron A triangular pyramid.

theorem A mathematical statement that can be proved to be true. Or sometimes a statement that is proposed and needs to be proved.

thousandths The place-value position in which a digit has a value equal to $\frac{1}{1,000}$ of itself; the third digit to the right of the decimal point.

3-dimensional (3-D) Solid objects that take up volume. 3-dimensional objects have length, width, and thickness.

time graph A graph that is constructed from a story that takes place over time. A time graph shows what has happened through a progression of time.

topologically equivalent In *topology*, a term for shapes that can be transformed into each other by a topological transformation. See also *topology*.

topology The study of the properties of shapes that are unchanged by shrinking, stretching, twisting, bending, and similar transformations. (Tearing, breaking, and sticking together, however, are not allowed.)

trade-first subtraction A subtraction method in which all trades are done before any subtractions are carried out.

transformation Something done to a geometric figure that produces a new figure. The most common transformations are *translations* (slides), *reflections* (flips), and *rotations* (turns). See also *isometry transformation*.

translation A movement of a figure along a straight line; a "slide."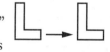

transversal A line that intersects two or more other lines.

trapezoid A quadrilateral that has exactly one pair of parallel sides.

trial-and-error method A method for finding the solution of an equation by trying several *test numbers*. See also *test number*.

triangular prism A prism whose bases are triangles.

triangular pyramid regular tetrahedron A pyramid in which all faces are triangles, any one of which can be called the base; also called a *tetrahedron*. If all of the faces are equilateral triangles, the pyramid is a regular tetrahedron.

truncate (1) To replace all of the digits to the right of a particular place with 0s. For example, 3,654 can be truncated to 3,650 or 3,600 or 3,000. Truncation is similar to rounding but is easier and always makes the number smaller (unless all the truncated digits are 0s). (2) To cut off a vertex of a solid figure.

turn See *rotation*.

turn-around facts A pair of multiplication (or addition) facts in which the order of the factors (or addends) is reversed. For example, 3 * 9 = 27 and 9 * 3 = 27 are turn-around multiplication facts, and 4 + 5 = 9 and 5 + 4 = 9 are turn-around addition facts. There are no turn-around facts for subtraction or division.

turn-around rule A rule for solving addition and multiplication problems based on the *commutative property*. For example, if you know that 6 * 8 = 48, then, by the turn-around rule, you also know that 8 * 6 = 48. See *commutative property*.

twin primes Two *prime numbers* that are separated by just one *composite number*. For example, 3 and 5 are twin primes; 11 and 13 are also twin primes.

2-dimensional (2-D) Having length and width but not thickness. 2-dimensional shapes have area but not volume. Circles and polygons are 2-dimensional.

unit A label used to put a number in context. In measuring length, for example, inches and centimeters are units. In "5 apples," the word *apples* is the unit. See also *whole*.

unit fraction A fraction whose numerator is 1. For example, $\frac{1}{2}$, $\frac{1}{3}$, $\frac{1}{8}$, and $\frac{1}{20}$ are unit fractions.

unit percent One percent (1%).

unit rate A *rate* with 1 in the numerator.

unlike denominators Denominators that are different, as in $\frac{1}{2}$ and $\frac{1}{3}$.

"unsquaring" a number Finding the *square root* of a number.

U.S. customary system of measurement The measuring system most frequently used in the United States.

vanishing line A line connecting a point on a figure in a *perspective drawing* with the *vanishing point*. See also *perspective drawing* and *vanishing point*.

vanishing point In a *perspective drawing*, the point at which parallel lines moving away from the viewer seem to converge. It is located on the *horizon line*. See also *perspective drawing* and *vanishing line*.

variable A letter or other symbol that represents a number. A variable can represent one specific number, or it can stand for many different numbers.

variable term A *term* that contains at least one variable.

Venn diagram A picture that uses circles or rings to show relationships between sets.

Girls on Sports Teams

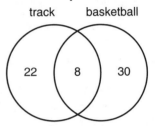

vertex The point where the rays of an angle, the sides of a polygon, or the edges of a polyhedron meet.

vertex point A point where corners of shapes in a *tessellation* meet. See also *tessellation*.

vertical Upright; perpendicular to the horizon.

vertical (or opposite) angles When two lines intersect, the angles that do not share a common side. Vertical angles have equal measures.

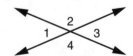

Angles 1 and 3 and Angles 2 and 4 are pairs of vertical angles.

volume The amount of space inside a 3-dimensional object. Volume is usually measured in cubic units, such as cubic centimeters or cubic inches. Sometimes volume is measured in units of capacity, such as gallons or liters.

whole (or ONE or unit) The entire object, collection of objects, or quantity being considered— the ONE, the unit, 100%.

whole number Any of the numbers 0, 1, 2, 3, 4, and so on.